IN VIEW OF THE TRADITION

In View of the Tradition

BLACK ART AND RADICAL THOUGHT

Roderick A. Ferguson

FORDHAM UNIVERSITY PRESS NEW YORK 2027

Visit us online at www.fordhampress.com.

For EU safety / GPSR concerns: Mare Nostrum Group B.V,
Doelen 72, 4831 GR Breda, The Netherlands,
gpsr@mare-nostrum.co.uk

Library of Congress Cataloging-in-Publication Data available online at https://catalog.loc.gov.

Printed in the United States of America
29 28 27 5 4 3 2 1
First edition

To all my kin and ancestors in the diaspora.
"Your work, that was done, to be done to be done to be done."
—Gwendolyn Brooks, "To the Diaspora"

Contents

Preface

I've been trying to figure out my relationship to art for quite some time. It begins, I think, when I started collecting Black art and realized that the works have a value beyond their prices. They are precious because of the histories they carry, the warnings they transmit, the meanings they receive, and the inspirations they offer like water to the thirsty.

A portion of this lesson can be found in the philosopher Walter Benjamin's 1931 essay "Unpacking My Library." About his and others' relationships to book collecting, he said, "The acquisition of books is by no means a matter of money."“[1] Instead, collecting is about the procuring of knowledge. He continued, "The period, the region, the craftsmanship, the former ownership—for a true collector the whole background of an item adds up to a magic encyclopedia whose quintessence is the fate of his object."[2] For Benjamin, the collector's excitement is wrapped in the wonder of the book's provenance—that record of the hands it passed through, the history that makes up the book's biography.

The discovery of the object's provenance becomes the basis of the collector's knowledge. Discussing this, Benjamin argues, "One only has to watch a collector handle the objects in his glass case. As he holds them in his hands, he seems to be seeing through them into their distant past as though inspired."[3] In this way, the collector is also the reader of the object, scrutinizing it for the mysteries of ownership: "According to the capabilities of the reader, books have their destinies."

Through collecting Black art, however, I soon discovered that there was more to my interest than who owned the mask, the shackle, or the poster. I was really intrigued by the histories that imbued the works—the hopes, fears, knowledges that were heaped on them, not only by their creators, but also by the worlds that once surrounded these objects. I was drawn to how the objects beckoned me to learn the contexts, ambitions, and apprehensions that occasioned them and how they did so not simply for their benefit but for my own.

How to read for those things became the driving question for me not simply as a collector but increasingly as a viewer. This book, in fact, is written with our capacities as observers in mind. What do modern and contemporary Black art hold for those who may never own these works but who have seen them in museums, art centers, galleries, magazines, public squares, and books? How might a viewer who has no collection use them to see a "distant past as though inspired"? How can we rally them for critical reflection and activation? These questions go far beyond the destiny of the object and in addition encompass the fate of the viewer. They require an understanding of what the objects mean for *our* critiques, politics, pasts, and futures.

Discussing the impact that collecting has on the owner, Benjamin said, "To a true collector, the acquisition of an old book is its rebirth. This is the childlike element which in a collector mingles with the element of old age. For children can accomplish the renewal of existence in a hundred unfailing ways."[4] This youthful wonder for the old can be a resource for our observer as well. For the engaged viewer, contemplating Black art can set in motion the rebirth of the artwork and its onlookers, a rebirth that allows viewers to see—with the freshness of a child—the histories, images, and knowledges that the artworks invoke. And seeing thus, the child can begin their maturation.

We might use Stephen Hayes's 2011 installation *Cash Crop* for such a rebirth. It consists of fifteen life-sized sculptures, depicting enslaved people of all ages from the middle passage. The figures are cast in concrete. Their hands and feet are shackled to metal chains and connected to a wooden pallet with the seal of the United States carved on it. Behind each figure is a long and cylindrical board on the back of which is the famous diagram of the *Brooks* ship from 1781. Depicting the ways that people were squeezed into the ship's bowels, abolitionists of the era used the illustration to

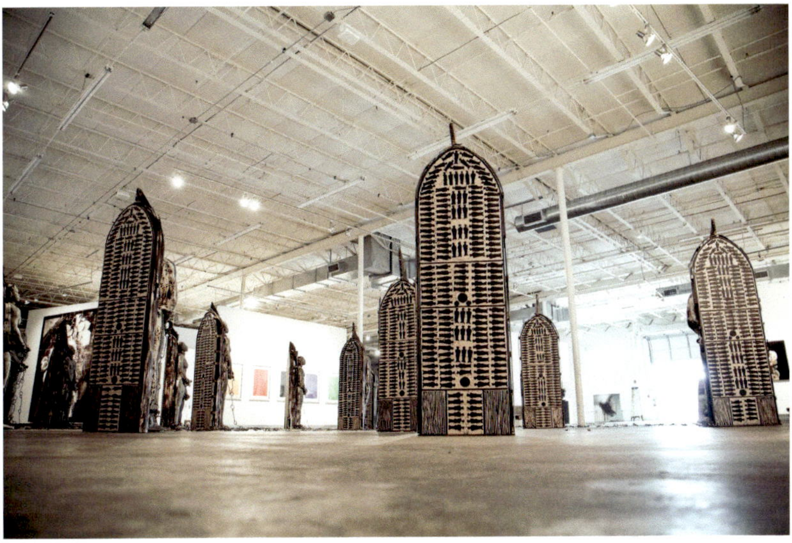

Figure 1. Stephen Hayes. *Cash Crop*. 2010. Fifteen life-sized mixed-media figures, with concrete, woodblock, iron. Durham, North Carolina. Reprinted with permission.

publicize the inhumanity of the trade. By placing the figures on the diagrammed boards, Hayes suggests that the lives of the transported were fashioned by the intersections of race and capitalism.

For Hayes, remembering the transatlantic slave trade provides a portal to global exploitations occurring in this moment. As he says, "When I looked at the *Brooks* slave ship plan, it kind of reminded me of a sweatshop in a third world country. If you take the top off a sweatshop in a third world country, it kind of looks like they've packed these people inside these sweatshops with just enough room to produce as much goods as possible."[5] Hence, in addition to being a depiction of the transatlantic slave trade, *Cash Crop* is a portal to other histories, cultures, and oppressions. The figures can thus be viewed as ancestors who stand at the doorway, encouraging us to make those connections.

It is not incidental that Hayes chose concrete as one of the materials for the installation. It is an immediately recognizable symbol of industry. As the art historian Cheryl Finley notes in her discussion of *Cash Crop*, "As Hayes puts it, 'You can come across [concrete] any day, all day long.'

The ubiquitous nature of this building material and its ability to withstand time also point to one of the key metaphors of *Cash Crop*: you can confront or be confronted by legacies of the transatlantic slave trade 'any day, all day long.'"[6] By using concrete, *Cash Crop* implies that slavery is literally written into the built environment and the economic products of the United States. Moreover, it suggests that the country and its wealth still depend upon hyperexploited labor.

To activate the installation's potential to reawaken us, we must allow ourselves to connect to it viscerally. Indeed, the figures in *Cash Crop* are trying to catch our attention. "As life-size figures," Finley says, "they stand eye to eye with the viewer, their expressions of pain and despair demanding an emotional connection with anyone who walks into the gallery."[7]

As a group, the men, women, and children in the installation invoke the underwater land where, according to vodou, the ancestors reside. As the filmmaker Maya Deren said in her classic book *Divine Horseman: The Living Gods of Haiti*, "One of the major Voudoun rituals is the ceremony of *retirer d'en bas de l'eau*, the reclamation of the soul of the deceased from the waters of the abyss, the world of les Invisibles."[8] Distinguishing this reclamation from nostalgia, Deren went on to say, "It is not a moment of return to the past; it is the procedure by which the race reincorporates the fruit of previous life processes into the contemporary moment, and so retains the past as the ground gained, upon and from which it moves forward to the future."[9] This recovery of ancestral knowledge and properties is intended for present-day utilization.

Hence, for our purposes, how we look at Black art can be that act of reincorporating and redeploying the fruits of prior struggles, histories, and cultures. We interpret Black art, therefore, not only to acquire knowledge but to revitalize agency. This is the tactical orientation of the viewer, an induction designed to elaborate the projects of freedom that the elders started and to look into one of the ways of emancipation.

IN VIEW OF THE TRADITION

Introduction

The Fool, the Trickster, and the Power of Áshe

This book is a fool's errand. To my knowledge, there is no text that asks Black visual art and Black radical literatures—in toto—to hold a mirror to one another. But what book, in its right mind, would attempt do so when art, in general, and Black art, in particular, seem so thoroughly caught in the commodity web of the market, making Black art's radical potential dubious at best? After all, in 2017, David Hammons's installation *Untitled* made of a basketball hoop and candelabras sold for over $8 million. That same year, Jean-Michel Basquiat's *Untitled* skull-painting sold for $150 million. In 2014, Chris Ofili's once controversial painting *Holy Virgin Mary* sold for $4.5 million dollars. These are only a few of the artworks by Black artists that are seemingly condemned by their price tags to be only the treasures of the wealthy rather than the tools of the insurgent.

So, if you were told that Black art can tell us something about the nature and possibilities of radicalism, why then would you waste your time? Hasn't art already discredited itself because of its reduction to dollar amounts? Hasn't it simply become part of the orgy of commodification, "[aiming] at nothing other than itself?"[1] And isn't the spectacular ascendancy of Black art in the art market a sign of its estrangement from, rather than its communion with, Black radical traditions?

There is reason to worry, to be sure. Indeed, when an artwork is reduced to its value on the market, all types of meanings, histories, and connections are lost. Those vanished elements make up the social character of an artwork—how the work imagines community and the social world; how it understands the relationship between the past, the present, and the future; and how it interprets the links between various forms of life.

Marx touched on this very thing when he said that as soon as a wooden table becomes more than something that people can use and instead becomes a thing exchanged on the market, it "transcends"[2] its identity as a sensible object, "[changing] into a thing."[3] Commodities begin to take on a life above and beyond the people, places, histories, and communities that produced them, and the social world begins to appear like "a relation between things"[4] rather than a relation between living beings. In those moments a great corruption has taken place, one in which people and communities are not understood to be the forces of history. Instead, markets and their products are taken to be the entities that move and shake the world. Rather than enriching our understanding of human and social possibility, commodification withers it.

When an artwork is known through its cost, its most important attribute becomes its price rather than the stuff that can yield other ways of knowing and encountering art—who made it, how it was made, under what conditions it was produced, what meanings it invokes, what alternative understandings and practices it can inspire, and what help it might provide. To the extent that we surrender to commodification's lie—that the artwork is the sum of the final bid, we rob ourselves of all the meanings that the work has to offer. In doing so, we raise the market's version of history to prominence and cast down the histories that brought the work into being in the first place.

Losing those histories and meanings is especially dangerous when it comes to Black art. Indeed, this book argues that because of the ongoing crises wrought by racism, colonialism, heteropatriarchy, capitalist inequality, environmental devastation, war, and so on, we need to clarify the social character of Black art in particular. Our task is not really a new one. In many ways, we are receiving a baton that has been passed from others in a very long relay. In 1956, for instance, the editors of the pan-African quarterly *Présence Africaine* argued that Black cultural workers were "under the duty to pay attention to all cultural production, to assess its trends and its possible effects, and to react accordingly."[5] Pointing to the ways that culture had been misused by politicians, princes, and emperors as a "buttress for their authority,"[6] the editors called on Black artists to make the "great problems"[7] of the world "accessible to every conscience."[8] They also summoned those artists to "reconstruct a world which is filled with life, thought, and passion and . . . [that thirsts] more than ever for justice, love, and peace."[9] Black artworks contain these histories and more, so how absurd to presume that their value can be squeezed into the boundaries of a price tag.

According to Cedric J. Robinson, who coined the term "the Black radical tradition," histories of anti-racist and anti-colonial social movements and writings by Black people cast doubt on the presumed power of capitalism to determine every ounce of life. This would lead Robinson to define the Black radical tradition as an accumulation of the histories of struggles and insurgencies that helped develop social consciousness and to promote and preserve the collective well-being of Black people, especially, and the world, generally.[10] This book attempts to create interpretations of Black art that will align with that aim.

The African American artist Elizabeth Catlett, for example, understood that if we wrested Black art from the meanings imposed upon it by the art market, we could arrive at something truly purposeful. She said, "If we can just get away from what's supposed to be the way of doing things, of doing the same fads in art and taking it to the galleries and charging higher and higher prices and creating less and less. And trying to be different, superficially, and ignoring our people, saying, 'We are artists, first, and then African Americans.'"[11] In a 1961 speech for the National Conference of Negro Artists, she continued this line of thinking and said, "It is . . . hard for an artist, conditioned to his dependence on art critics and galleries and dealers, to think of the art he produces objectively, to think of his individual position in a historic period of time. We need to reevaluate and determine what is trivial and what is vital. We live in an environment that emphasizes material possessions, that reduces living and life to a level of minor importance."[12]

For Catlett, the market potentially jeopardizes the historical forcefulness of Black art. It can present Black culture as a tool for the superficial purposes of commodification. It can cause artists to identify more with the market and its preoccupations than with the travails and hopes of actual Black cultures. It can lead us to lose a sense of our place in history. As a result, the substance of life is downgraded as the market confounds our sense of what is vital.

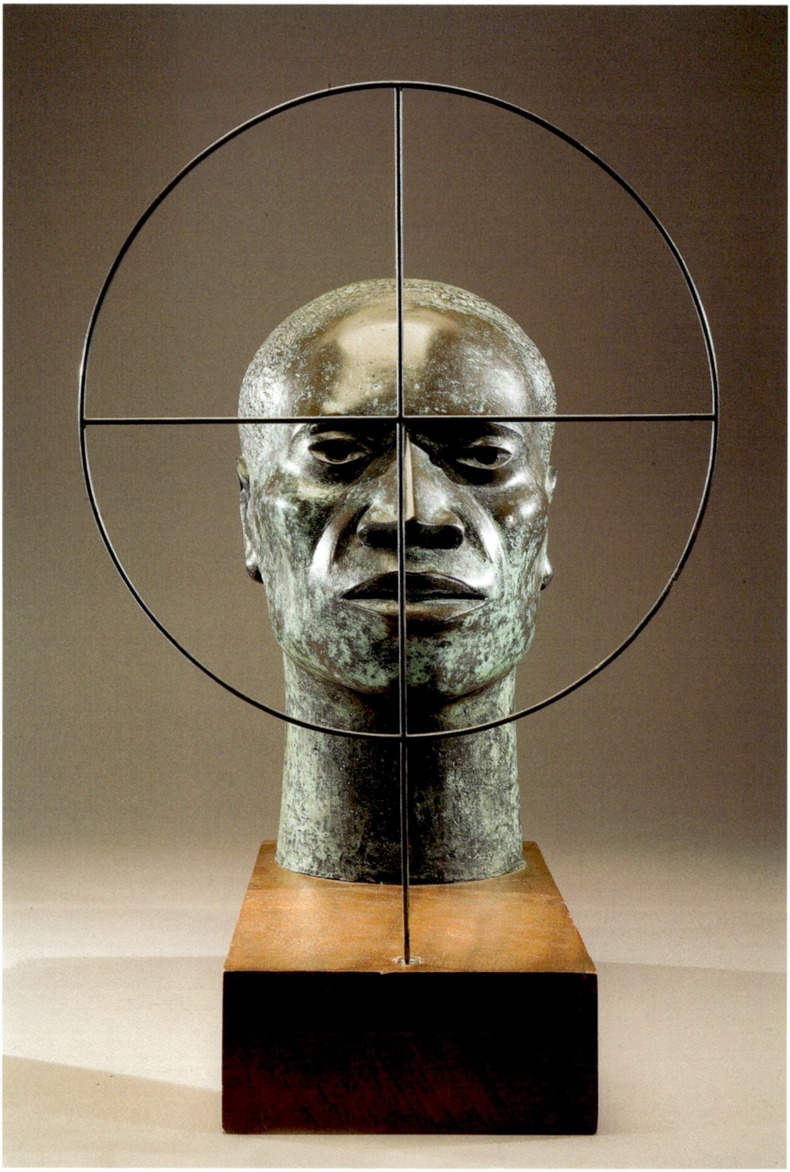

Figure 2. Elizabeth Catlett. *Target*. 1970. Bronze. Courtesy of the Amistad Research Center, New Orleans, LA. © 2024 Mora-Catlett Family / Licensed by VAGA at Artists Rights Society (ARS), NY. Photo: Courtesy of the Amistad Research Center, New Orleans, LA / Bridgeman Images.

In a world seemingly captured by the market, what chance is there to reclaim Black art as a compass for determining which routes enhance social life versus which roads diminish it? In his classic book, *The Gift: Creativity and the Artist in the Modern World*, Lewis Hyde argues, "[A] work of art is a gift, not a commodity."[13] Clarifying, he goes on to say, "[Works] of art exist simultaneously in two 'economies,' a market economy and a gift economy. Only one of these is essential, however: a work of art can survive without the market, but where there is no gift there is no art."[14] For Hyde, works of art are the artists' gifts to their audiences. As gifts, the artworks constrain commodification even as they are marketed. Because of their "outer lives"—the ways that artworks affect us—the heart is moved, the soul is revived, the senses are delighted, and courage is awakened. Because of art's ability to illuminate our inner talents, it exceeds the merely financial possibilities of property.

For Black art, the stakes are even larger than those of art in general. Black art involves gifts given in the context of the ongoing legacies of slavery, colonialism, racial segregation, apartheid, and their impacts on class, gender, and sexuality. I insist, then, that Black art can remind us of histories and connections that we need to remember and know. Black art can also renew our sense that life can be redrawn, revalued, re-sculpted, and redesigned. In sum, Black art has gifted us with a powerful discernment, one that declares, "even during the storm and the night/ for us there is plenty of light here."[15]

If the market rips Black art out of its social and historical contexts and meanings, then alternatively we might engage Black art as a gift that can inspire us to connect struggles that are seemingly disconnected and to strive toward the full potential of liberatory agendas. In this instance, Black art takes on a comprehensive meaning, one in which the artwork becomes a map toward the higher ground. It is what permits us to place Black art alongside the traditions of Black radicalism. As both can be powerful ways of asking what is vital in life, this book puts the two in conversation to raise Black, human, and planetary existence to a level of major importance.

But the art world is contradictory. It's not only made up of auctions and deals. It is also composed of curators, collectors, critics, intellectuals, artists, journals, and exhibitions that try to create alternative ways to hold and conceptualize artworks. Put another way, the art world is the location for the turning of the artwork into a commodity, but it is also the territory in which art can take on the attributes of the gift. This book is inspired by the latter.

You can probably already tell that this book is a fool's endeavor, not only because it believes that even in the midst of these contradictions art is still within reach of radical visions. It is also foolish because it holds fast to the idea that a truly Black radical practice means developing—difficult though it may be—some fluency with Black histories and struggles around the globe. Necessarily then, this book understands "Black" to mean more than "African American." It harkens back to an earlier moment in which "Black" was not only a way of assigning beauty but was also a means of connecting the global north to the global south and of dealing with the legacies of colonialism within a nation's borders. Looking to the associations between Black art and Black radical traditions allows us to reckon with the ways that both compel us to strive for lives and interests that are far-reaching.

This is not a small job, particularly in a US context in which African American art, history, and political struggles have become the privileged location in which to define and interpret Blackness across the globe. This privileging of US Blacks obscures the wealth and complexities of Black culture, politics, and intellect produced by Black peoples outside the United States. In a discussion about the significance of contemporary African art, for instance, the late Nigerian curator and theorist Okwui Enwezor and the Nigerian art historian and curator Chika Okeke-Agulu write, "Whether or not their works require close reading to tease out their central subject, what is certain is that contemporary African artists . . . contribute to debates about the fate and experiences of the late twentieth-century Africa, its constituent states, and peoples."[16] If we privilege African American experiences, then we will miss out on debates like the ones that Enwezor and Okeke-Agulu invoke.

The privileging of African Americans has a long history that this book tries to forgo. For instance, the scholar Alain Locke in his classic 1925 essay "The New Negro" defined the global significance of African Americans by saying, "With the American negro, his new internationalism is primarily an effort to recapture contact with the scattered peoples of African derivation."[17] But for Locke, African Americans had a presumed advantage over their Black siblings around the world. African Americans, he said, acted as the "*advanced-guard of the African peoples* in their contact with Twentieth-century civilization" (emphasis mine). Invoking Marcus

Garvey's back to Africa movement, Locke wrote, "Garveyism may be a transient, if spectacular, phenomenon, but the possible role of the American Negro in the future development of Africa is one of the most constructive and universally helpful missions that any modern people can lay claim to." Here, Locke constructs African Americans as a modernizing force for an "underdeveloped" territory and people. Like secular missionaries, they would apparently bring civilization to Black people on the continent. In this book, I mean to disrupt this construction and the privileges it suggests.

To this end, the book attempts to remind readers of the global and diasporic stakes of Black radical traditions and the necessary place that art must have in those concerns. It asserts that a fully achieved Black radical interpretation of art means identifying the global stakes of artworks often presumed to be national. Those global markings are merely the artistic counterparts to the ways that Black peoples are marked by global forces. The Afro-Latine curator Ariana Curtis identifies, for example, how ethnic diversities imprint Black cultures within the United States. She writes, "The same waves of decolonization, African and Caribbean independence, and Black immigration in the '60s, '70s, and '80s that reshaped the lexicon of global Black identities also diversified the reality of Black ethnicities within the United States."[18] Decolonization, independence, and migration would also be the fields from which new affinities and paradigms would be grown and harvested. Perhaps gesturing toward these historical processes, the art historian and writer Kobena Mercer argues, "[African American, Black British, and Caribbean artists] brought renewed urgency to our understanding of art and society in an era of globalization."[19] Calling Black art and Black radical traditions to the table can be one way to illuminate the global stakes of both.

Still, this book is a fool's undertaking. It's not just because of its belief that there is a conversation already going on between Black art and Black radicalism, and it's not merely because of its conviction that they can inspire us to be fluent in histories of Blackness that are different from our own. It is a fool's quest for yet another reason. Blackness is often discussed in this moment as an ideal that is so exceptional that it has no relation to other histories, cultures, and forms of difference. In contrast (and truthfully in opposition) to this sentiment, this book insists that Blackness is nothing if not relational. Hence, *In View of the Tradition* argues that one of the most prominent and powerful currents within Black radical traditions is its emphasis on the need for dialogue with other cultural and political histories. Indeed, the book contends that this dialogical nature is the foundation of Black radical traditions and Black art.

The book also turns to Black art to confront urgent issues that might otherwise go unaddressed in Black political discourse. In this way, it takes particular inspiration from Black queer, trans, and feminist cultural work. These cultural workers have often used their work to identify issues that are frequently evaded, denied, and suppressed. Here we might think of the work of such artists as Ajamu, Sonia Boyce, Renee Cox, Rotimi Fani-Kayode, Lubaina Himid, Lyle Ashton Harris, Isaac Julien, Tiona Nekkia McClodden, Kara Walker, and so on. We can derive insights from the British Nigerian queer artist Fani-Kayode, who wrote, "Both aesthetically and ethically, I seek to translate my rage and my desire into new images which will undermine conventional perceptions and which may reveal hidden worlds."[20] We could also turn to the words of the South African artist Zanele Muholi. They produced the 2006 photographic series *Faces and Phases* to respond to the erasure of Black lesbians in accounts of South Africa's anti-apartheid, feminist, and queer movements and to the violence visited upon Black lesbians and Black gender queer people. About the need for the series, Muholi wrote, "It is important to mark, map, and preserve our mo(ve)ments through visual histories for reference and posterity so that future generations will note that we were here."[21]

Black feminist, queer, and trans artists have demonstrated the ability of visual art to engage the unspeakable not only in the general society but within Black communities and critical domains as well. The artwork that this book addresses is not necessarily feminist or queer, but the book takes these feminist, queer, and trans formations as crucial components of Black radical traditions. Moreover, they inform the book's analyses.

So, if you suspect that the book travels beyond those Black radical traditions that simply engage capitalism, then you're right. Indeed, the Black radical traditions that I'm referring to are the ones that presume not only the critique of capital but also those that mandate deep literacy about all social formations. These are the critical traditions that critique nationalist formations, that analyze gender and sexual regulations, and that examine how Black poor and working-class communities are pathologized. They are also the Black radical traditions that assert that the struggles of

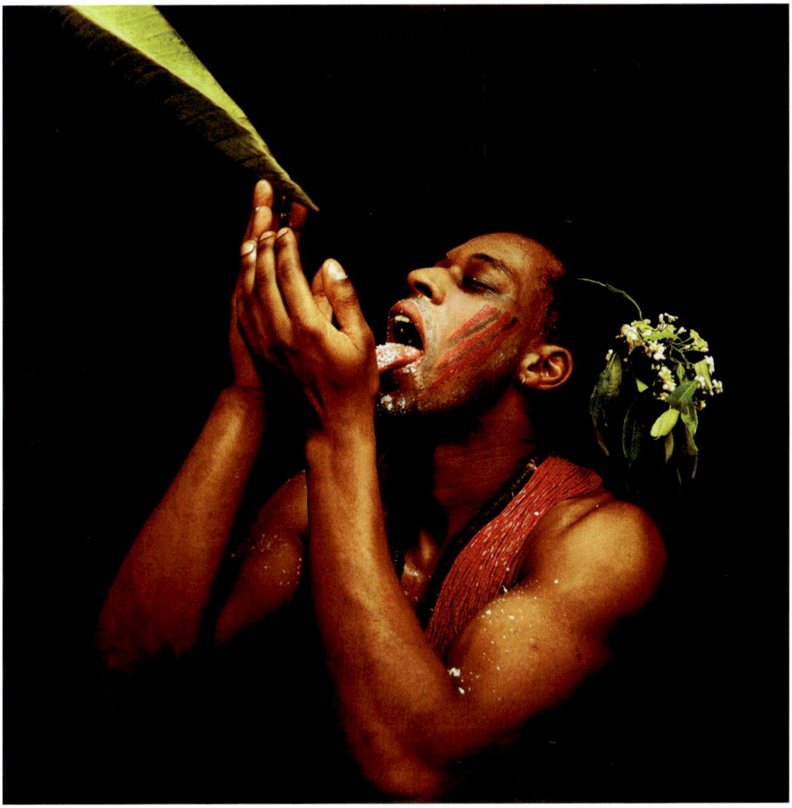

Figure 3. Rotimi Fani-Kayode. *Nothing to Lose VII (Bodies of Experience)*. 1989. Autograph, London. Reprinted with permission.

other cultures matter for Black radicalism and that the sanctity and protection of the planet are paramount. Hence, the book deploys a Black radicalism that borrows from Black intellectual traditions that engage Marxist, feminist, queer, and environmentalist genealogies. The book celebrates a Black radical universe that is always growing.

In fact, one of the ways that we can expand the Black radical universe is by heeding Black modern and contemporary art. What would happen, for instance, if we used Black art to explore the role of settler colonialism in US society and in African American history? How would our appreciation for Black art and Black radicalism change if we saw war and environmental devastation in Africa and elsewhere as both an artistic and political concern? When Black artists address global migration, how does the remit of Black radicalism change at that moment? What would happen if we used Black art to see—I mean really see—poor and working-class Black people for all the complexities that they embody? And how could all this result in a fuller notion of what it means to be human in the twenty-first century?

This book by no means presents the artists and the issues that it discusses as an exhaustive list of the cultural workers or concerns that should be addressed. Instead, it tries to model how we can grow the list of items and cultural forms that Black radical politics can and should tend to. The issues and artists that I have chosen are simply some of the ones who have captivated me the most for this book's interventions. But there are, of course, others. Some of the other artists that I have admired, studied, taught and written about are Igshaan Adams, Omar Ba, Sokari Douglas Camp, Maria Magdalena Campos-Pons, Emory Douglas, Fowokan, Nicholas Hlobo, Clotilde Jiménez, Claudette Johnson, Titus Kaphar, Toyin Ojih-Odutola, Athi-Patra Ruga, Keith Piper, Zina Saro-Wiwa, the Otolith Group, Daniel Lind-Ramos, Tschabalala Self, Adejoke Tubiyele, Lynette Yiadom-Boakye, and so on. There are also so many other issues that I hope will be researched in texts that will emanate from this one—prison-industrial expansion, homophobia, transphobia, islamophobia, genocide, neocolonialism, hegemonic masculinity, Afro-Latinidad, and so on. The book is merely intended as one model of how the search for Black radicalism's overlaps with Black diasporic art might take place. My greatest desire is that additional models might spring into being.

In keeping with this foolish errand, Chapter 1 analyzes the work of the assemblage artist Noah Purifoy, the Watts rebellion, and the exhibition—*66 Signs of Neon*—that came out of that uprising. The chapter situates Purifoy, the rebellion, and the exhibition in a global discourse that understood Black people to be artistic beings, regardless of rank or profession. Specifically, I show how the people of Watts took care of and created art and how their stewardship of it rebuked government's and media's framing of the people as looters, rioters, and good-for-nothings. Focusing on the Watts rebellion and the art that came from it gives us a sense of a little-appreciated moment in history, one in which modern art was not something withheld from or given to the people. It was something that they midwifed into being despite all that the city officials believed about them. Hence, the chapter demonstrates how the category "artist" was more than a technical category. It was part of a global ethos in which Black artists and intellectuals understood the making of culture as the remaking of the world and addressed Black people as having the power to make things happen.

Chapter 2 examines artist Carrie Mae Weems's *The Hampton Project*. This installation depicted the buried and controversial history of how predominantly Black Hampton Institute (now Hampton University) was the location for an assimilationist project for African Americans and a settler colonial project for Native Americans, projects that would attempt to turn both groups into proper citizen-laborers. In examining this history, the chapter deals with the simultaneous training of Blacks and Native peoples into the norms of American and Western civilization. The chapter argues that the different procedures by which the students were socialized into dominant ideologies cannot be understood without an appreciation of their overlaps. Chapter 2 provides a reckoning with the bourgeois and settler-colonial implications of Black intellectual life and work and sees that reckoning as necessary for Black radical politics.

Chapter 3 pivots to artists and art works that have addressed the sea as a site of colonial, imperial, and capitalist expansion and exploitation. Attending to the works of John Akomfrah, Hew Locke, and Fabrice Monteiro, this chapter investigates the role that the sea has played in the constitution of Black identities, neocolonialism, and racial capitalism. Moreover, the chapter analyzes the effect that this role has had on transnational migration, refugeeism, and environmental devastation. The chapter deals with the sea as the contemporary transit route for folks from the Caribbean and Africa as well as the graveyard for enslaved people and migrants. Chapter 3 ponders what a focus on the sea might mean for expanding the geopolitical imagination of Black radical traditions and for widening the peoples and urgencies those traditions must engage.

Chapter 4 focuses on the work of the Kenyan American artist Wangechi Mutu. It looks at the disturbing beauty of Mutu's collage work and uses that work to disinter the violence that links colonialism and anti-colonial struggle, a violence that shapes the postcolonial period. It puts Mutu's art in conversation with the work of Black feminists who write about Africa to bedevil conventional and progressive arguments about the role of violence in war and struggle. Focusing on Mutu's collages, the chapter shows how African women who have survived war and violence have pieced new worlds into being.

The conclusion views Cauleen Smith's *Human 3.0 Reading List*. The installation is composed of fifty-seven book covers that Smith drew herself. *Human 3.0* is—in Smith's words—a "low-grade inoculation" against neoliberalism and its effects on Black communities and the world. The conclusion analyzes this work to assert the importance of Black radical traditions as diverse and living projects, ones that include but are not exhausted by the works of Black authors and artists, ones that are populated by an ever-growing list of authors, texts, artists, images, and struggles. The conclusion argues that Black radical traditions can only be realized through a constant bibliophilic immersion and production into the vast and unfolding intellectual, historical, and geopolitical genealogies of Black radical traditions. The conclusion maintains that such an immersion and literacy are required to meet our myriad existential and social emergencies.

This book is a fool's mission, and to complete its assignment, it mobilizes the unique powers of the fool. In various mythologies, the fool is the boundary-breaker, the irreverent one, and the transgressive sage. Having little in the way of possessions, the fool learns whatever they can on the journey. As a figure that moves through the pages of this book, the fool calls for Black radical traditions ready to confront not only the contradictions that make up external forces but the ones that constitute Black radicalism as well.

Foolishly, the book activates that quality of folk wisdom that stands in contrast to the workings of market forces. Like the artworks it addresses, I offer the book as a gift as well. Whether as food, art, flowers, herbs, feasts, fertility, or personal sacrifice, the gift, according to Hyde, is formed and circulated within a "spiritual or psychological commerce."[22] In folklore, the gift reveals the deeper meanings of life and requires honest self-assessments.

The art historian Robert Farris Thompson said in his classic study *Flash of the Spirit: African and Afro-American Art and Philosophy* that the Yoruba "show their special concern for the proprieties of right living through their worship of major gods and goddesses."[23] Each of those deities, according to Thompson, is "essentially a unique manifestation of áshe, the power to make things happen, a key to futurity and self-realization in Yoruba terms."

Áshe is not only a property of Yoruba deities though. It can also be found in artworks as well. As Thompson says, "A thing or work of art that has áshe transcends ordinary questions about its makeup and confinements: it is divine force incarnate."[24]

Although I borrow from Thompson's discussion, my own use of it attempts to engage it for its political possibilities. Hence, the concept—as I use it—suggests the power to imagine new political and social worlds. In doing so, this book tries to find the traces of áshe in Black art and Black radical writings. Thus it searches for those elements within cultural works that point us to our capacities to make things happen so that we are in right relation with the world. Although the principle of áshe is grounded in Yoruba culture, it conforms to ideas in other contexts. Discussing the illuminative capacity of art, Hyde, for instance, says, "We may not have the power to profess our gifts as the artist does, and yet we come to recognize, and in a sense to receive, the endowments of our being through the agency of his creation."[25] Put in the terms of áshe, art—for Hyde—can be a way of acquainting us with our own powers of manifestation.

In addition, Aristotle argued that every art involves "bringing something into being."[26] For him, artistic production and politics fall under this definition because both politics and art involve developing the right dispositions to bring things into the world.[27] As these examples from African and Western contexts suggest, the push to develop our capacities to usher things into existence crosses spiritual, political, and artistic orders. And as this book focuses on Black diasporic art and Black radical traditions, it does so to inspire us to cause a fully just and liberated world to come into form. The áshe of Black diasporic art and Black radical traditions compels us to reclaim our historical agency and social consciousness and to do so against those social forces that would dry them up.

In many ways, áshe is a fool's prerogative and power. In Yoruba cosmology, Eshu is the prankster-god, and divine creative energy was first manifested through him.[28] Eshu is many things—the god of crossroads and intersections; he is all genders; he is navel, womb, and phallus. The people know him also as the one who uses tomfoolery to transgress and inspire transgression. Thompson tells us that "[Eshu] sometimes even 'wears' the crossroads as a cap, colored Black on one side, red on the other, provoking in his wake foolish arguments about whether his cap is black or red, wittily insisting by implication that we view a person or a thing from all sides before we form a general judgment."[29] Eshu is the learned and agentive fool, the one who both ushers things into being and promotes the comprehensive meaning as the only real truth.

Through Eshu we can find encouragement for this book's intended audience—the young reader who is interested in addressing systems of injustice and devising alternatives to them. The reader of this book may not know about art, Black art, or Black radical histories, but they are interested in what these things stand for—the need and right to make worlds that are beautiful and just and the understanding that improving the world means considering the limitations of the worlds that we have. Whoever holds this book—I figure—will be like the best of students—ready for the day's lesson. They will not look away.

In folklore, fools like Eshu have had many guises. Some say the fool is a beggar. Others say, no, they are Anansi, Brer Rabbit, and the old lady that lives near the woods. Most will say, though, that the fool is the one who will volunteer to lose their innocence so that they might attain wisdom. So let this book be a fool's adventure for you. Let us try—as best we can—to find the signs of wisdom and intelligence on the works that we chance upon. Let us learn their secrets. The conversations between Black radical traditions and Black diasporic art can offer us more than social and artistic analyses. They can give us a renewed sense of the meaning and purpose of life. Foolish as it may sound, there is plenty here to sustain and build a wisdom culture.

1
The Shit, the World, and Their Remaking
Noah Purifoy

There are those who remember that before 107th Street was cluttered with police, the military, and Molotov cocktails, artwork had happened there. Noah Purifoy recollected that he and the others who worked at the Watts Towers Art Center had a clear view of all aspects of the rebellion—the fires that fought the sky and the smoke that filled it. And then there were the people who looted the buildings—a few of them students of Purifoy's who deposited their bounty in and around the center. About this, he said, "We permitted that, because this was an extremely unique experience, and we thought at least the kids were still interested in what was happening at the center."[1]

Reflecting on his time as director of the Watts Towers Art Center from 1962 until shortly after the Watts Rebellion in 1965, the artist Noah Purifoy said this about the artistic programs that he and his friends—the arts educator Sue Welch and the artist Judson Powell—developed there: "We believed that an art experience was transferrable to other areas of their activity and so forth and that if they could come to the [Watts] Tower and have a good experience, a positive experience, they could take this experience with them wherever they go."[2]

Some five years before Purifoy's directorship and during the wake of independence in Africa and the Caribbean, the Martinican writer and poet Aimé Césaire delivered a speech at the Second Congress of Negro

Writers and Artists. Sounding a note similar to Purifoy's, he said, "In short, even inside the colonial system itself [cultural work] restores historic initiative to those whom it has been the mission of the colonial system to deprive of all historic initiative."[3] Both Césaire's and Purifoy's pronouncements come out of periods of racial and neocolonial subjugation. Both also suggest that cultural and artistic production are powerful means for the downtrodden to claim their right to remake the world.

The art that Purifoy fostered and made was in dialogue with ideas like Césaire's, ideas central to Black radical traditions. The idea that everyday people, especially Blacks, could approach the world like artists and could remake it was a basic tenet of Black radical writings and the assemblage art that Purifoy created. As such, this idea flew in the face of official notions about Black cultural dysfunction and inferiority, notions promoted by various levels and forms of government and even by Purifoy himself.

Whether it was coming from visual art or from Black radical writings, the idea that Black communities were not only troubled but imaginative locales represented an attempt to shift how Black communities and peoples would be both understood *and* seen. That shift took place in the mid to late '60s, which saw urban uprisings, the emergence of Black power, the Black arts movement, and the struggles against colonialism and neocolonialism. Black artists and intellectuals in the global north and the global south responded to those conditions with cultural work that would attempt to illuminate and promote Black communities and peoples as generators of that work. In opposition to how racial discourses were interpreting and representing Black peoples, the moment of anti-racist and anti-colonial agitation epitomized an attempt to provide alternative ways of understanding and seeing Black populations. Purifoy's work and the Watts neighborhood were part of that effort.

Much has been written about Watts and the rebellion that took its name—the socioeconomic conditions that led to it, the devastation that defined it, and the lives ended because of it. But the refuse of that rebellion—specifically, the junk that Noah Purifoy gathered into art—was the basis of a poetic rediscovery of a neighborhood and its people, a rediscovery that was the local instantiation of a global and diasporic rethinking.

"An Insensate Rage of Destruction": How the Officials Saw the People

On August 24, 1965, Governor Edmund G. Brown of California commissioned a group of white and Black leaders to "make an objective and dispassionate study of the Los Angeles riots."[4] The committee would be made up of "distinguished Californians" hailing from clerical, corporate, and academic sectors. The report was officially titled *Violence in the City—An End or a Beginning?* but it was known as *The McCone Report* after the committee chairman, John A. McCone, the former director of Central

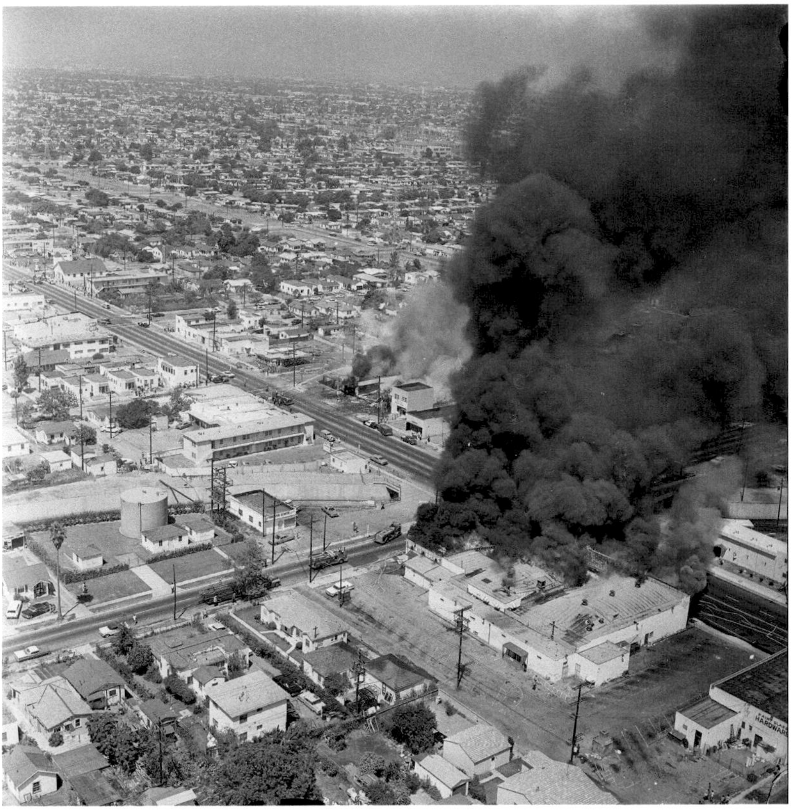

Figure 4. Watts Uprising. Public domain.

Intelligence. The report would introduce the rebellion, which was spurred by the arrest of a Black youth for drunk driving, this way: "In the ugliest interval, which lasted from Thursday through Saturday, perhaps as many as 10,000 Negroes took to the streets in marauding bands."[5] The report continued by describing the crowd's allegedly greedy aggression: "They looted stores, set fires, beat up white passersby whom they hauled from stopped cars, many of which were turned upside down and burned, exchanged shots with law enforcement officers, and stoned and shot at firemen. The rioters seemed to be caught up in an insensate rage of destruction."[6]

This story of "insensate rage" obscured years of "intense racial and class segregation, miserable schools, and large-scale joblessness"[7] for the neighborhood's Black population. In addition to increasing unemployment, Watts also suffered from "decreased rates of homeownership, and the loss of a once superb public transportation system in favor of private automobiles and freeways that cut across the residential area,"[8] according to the historian Sarah Schrank. These structural inequalities would collude with a climate of fear and intimidation produced by the police. As historian Donna Murch argues, "A hostile and overwhelmingly white police force engaged in routine traffic stops of motorists of color, beatings of neighborhood residents, and the harassment of interracial couples."[9] While the committee presented the report as "an accurate chronology and description of the riots,"[10] it would be a powerful tool in teaching people how to see and how *not* to see the rebellion and Watts's Black community.

The report begins by coaxing readers to see the city's Black migrants within a familiar tale of newcomers who have failed to assimilate into the larger culture. As the report stated, "These riots were each a symptom of a sickness at the center of our cities. In almost every major city, Negroes pressing ever more densely into the central city and occupying areas from which Caucasians have moved in their flight to the suburbs have developed an isolated existence with a feeling of separation from the community as a whole."[11] Suggesting that at least some of the insurgency arose from the presumed backwardness of the Black community, the report went on to argue, "Many have moved to the city only in the last generation and are totally unprepared to meet the conditions of modern city life."[12] Coupled with the economic and social deprivation of the neighborhoods, this alleged backwardness would lead to a tangle of pathologies that came to signify the meaning of Black urban communities. As the commission stated, "At the core of the cities where they cluster, law and order have only a tenuous hold; the conditions of life itself are often marginal; idleness leads to despair and finally, mass violence supplies a momentary relief from the malaise."[13] Whether consciously or not, the McCone Report was educating the public in how to see US Black communities and the insurrections that were occurring in many of them.

Rather than a simple description of the causes of the rebellion, the report was more like a manual that attempted to train city officials, civic leaders, and residents in how to look at and thereby process the uprising. Writing about the ways in which "race is a matter of looking,"[14] visual culture scholar Shawn Michelle Smith argues that "looking is learned" and "seeing is coded in terms of race."[15] This implies that looking is a practice that we are socialized into rather than a gesture that we do naturally. In other words, the report was teaching people where to look—at the cultural backgrounds of the people in Watts, at the community's roots as migrants from the American South, at their family structures, and at the social dysfunction within their communities. It was encouraging readers to see those elements as signs of Black people's presumed cultural and racial backwardness and deviation.

Along these lines, the McCone Report not only constructed a story about Black urban life. It also installed a set of images about that life and its consequences for US social order. Discussing the ways in which texts teach us how to see, Smith writes, "Although rarely considered visual culture beyond incursions of visual description, literature is a key site through which looking is learned and viewing subjects are produced."[16] On first blush, the McCone Report does not appear to be a part of visual culture, but inasmuch as it was training its readers to see Black people and communities in a particular way, the report proved itself to be a key component in the visual production of race, producing people who would look at Black communities in certain ways.

The Re-seeing of 107th Street

Purifoy himself often looked at Black people in stereotypical manners. He believed that Blacks had short attention spans, that poor people and African Americans had "a tendency to not want to relate to each other on an equal level." Black people, he said, "were inclined to be selfish and vindictive, often childlike, as the case may be."[17] Indeed, he saw things the way the report did, stating initially that he and Powell "thought it a good report—that it advocated most things necessary for the betterment of the community. However, we observed that there was no mention of art education."[18]

Although Purifoy's beliefs may not have always resonated with the writers and artists that hailed from Black radical traditions, his work and the people that inspired it certainly did. The Watts Arts Center was the first arts education project to cover multiple genres in South Los Angeles.[19] Once, while working as the director of the center, he convened a project in which he, volunteers, and young people from the community took paint donated by the city's stores and painted all the houses on 107th street. Afterward, they "washed the street down" and held a block party. Describing that day, he said, "The whole community came. The streets were so crowded we had to spend most of our time directing traffic. For the open house, as we called it, we erected a mural outside with some painting and sculpture and whatnot."[20] He summed up the meaning of that day and what it meant to him as the director by saying, "This was the highlight of my experience there, an extremely profound experience."[21]

The profundity of the story lies in the fact that the people, the ones who—according to the report were "unprepared for the modern"—were wholly involved in a contemporary art project, demonstrating that there is no antithesis between art and the so-called Black underclass. Because of this, the 107th Street installation represented a radically democratic vision of contemporary art but not one initiated or governed by the state. Instead, it was completely driven by the people from the neighborhood itself.

This story of the wonder that unfurled on 107th Street resonates with an argument that the writer Lorraine Hansberry offered in 1959. In a speech titled "The Negro Writer and His Roots: Towards a New Romanticism," she argued that the task of the Black writer in the mid-twentieth century was to "turn . . . inward toward our people and their complex and still transitory culture."[22] Describing this inward turn, she went on to say, "There is much to celebrate, there always has been. We have given the world many of its heroes and the marching feet have not stopped yet. Turn inward to where a culture has never, as Alain Locke pointed out thirty years ago, been adequately understood."[23] Hansberry's speech suggests that there exists an irreducible complexity to Black life, one in which everyday people could reclaim a neighborhood from blight and give themselves and others a sense of how democratic and artful life can be. The labor of the 107th Street volunteers went beyond simply beautifying property that was probably in need of an uplift. It was in fact an effort to help rouse the life of the community itself. The installation promoted a vision of the artist as the creator of an alternative collective and public space, one in which the artist's powers were extended to very practical ends, ones that involved doing what the city refused to do and could not imagine—produce a Black world that was artful, joyful, and livable.

The Global Mood of 107th Street

It is important to note that the transformation of 107th Street took place within a change in the global mood. This was a moment in which Black artists and intellectuals were aggressively reinterpreting the significance of everyday Black peoples and cultures. For instance, the editors of the Black francophone journal *Presence Africaine* asserted in 1956, "Culture is no longer a distinctive decoration reserved for themselves by a handful of elect, nor an activity for the luxurious alone."[24] Artistic culture, according to them, was becoming more accessible and powerful for how Black artists in particular did and understood their work. As they said, "Under the pressure of events creative artists are coming down from their ivory tower and giving themselves up to social problems."[25] As Purifoy tried to make formal art available to people in Watts, people who were already immersed in an aesthetic existence, he was in fact, taking part in what the *Presence Africaine* editors were describing.

This global mood was one in which culture was understood as something shaped by many hands. As the editors put it, "We are tending toward the totalization of cultural consciousness. . . . [The] acquisition of traditional knowledge is sometimes less important than the creation (or the action, or the work) which answers to the current problems of mankind."[26] This was fundamentally a sea change in how Black communities throughout the world were seen and comprehended. Instead of being regarded as history's bystanders, Black people would be understood as part of the great momentum of history. If documents like the McCone Report were teaching people how to see Blacks, those documents were set against a diasporic atmosphere that was attempting to educate people to see Black cultures as participants in history's highest dramas. Artistic cultures were crucial to that effort.

During the period of the Watts rebellion, art was vital to how Black people in the neighborhood saw and valued themselves. For instance, in addition to leaving unharmed the white businesses that treated them fairly, the rebels—as the historian Gerald Horne noted—left the Watts Towers unscathed as well. The Towers were created by the white Italian immigrant and Watts Resident Sabato "Sam" Rodia and were viewed by the Black residents as a source of pride and identity. By leaving the Towers undamaged, the people were showing that their ire was directed toward the symbols of their racial and economic alienation and not at the buildings and artworks that reflected their self-worth and collective belonging.

A few of the so-called "rioters," Purifoy remembered, were the art students themselves. Recalling that moment, he said, "The students at the towers—particularly the adolescents—participated in the riot. Most everyone did. They would loot and stash their loot in and around the center." Defying the conventional image of rioters, the students took their bounty to the art center rather than home, proof for Purifoy that the center had become "a place for them, a center for them, a refuge, so to speak."[27] Far from being a story of rebels who devalued a neighborhood, Purifoy's memory shows how in this case several of the rebels were in fact the artists who raided the streets and buildings in order to build the community anew.

In her address, Hansberry identified the duty of the Black artist as "the vast task of cultural and historical reclamation."[28] In light of her assertion, we can see the rebellion as a moment of reclamation rather than vandalism, a reclamation that required the demolition of property and its alienations. In *The Economic and Philosophic Manuscripts*, Karl Marx said that the value of workers decreases in "direct proportion to the increasing value of the world of things."[29] For Marx, the more commodities and private property were valued, the more the worker was debased. For the people who participated in the rebellion, destroying the property was also an attempt to strike out against their debasement.

For Black populations the world over, segregated property was not the only source of alienation. Colonized property alienated Blacks in Africa

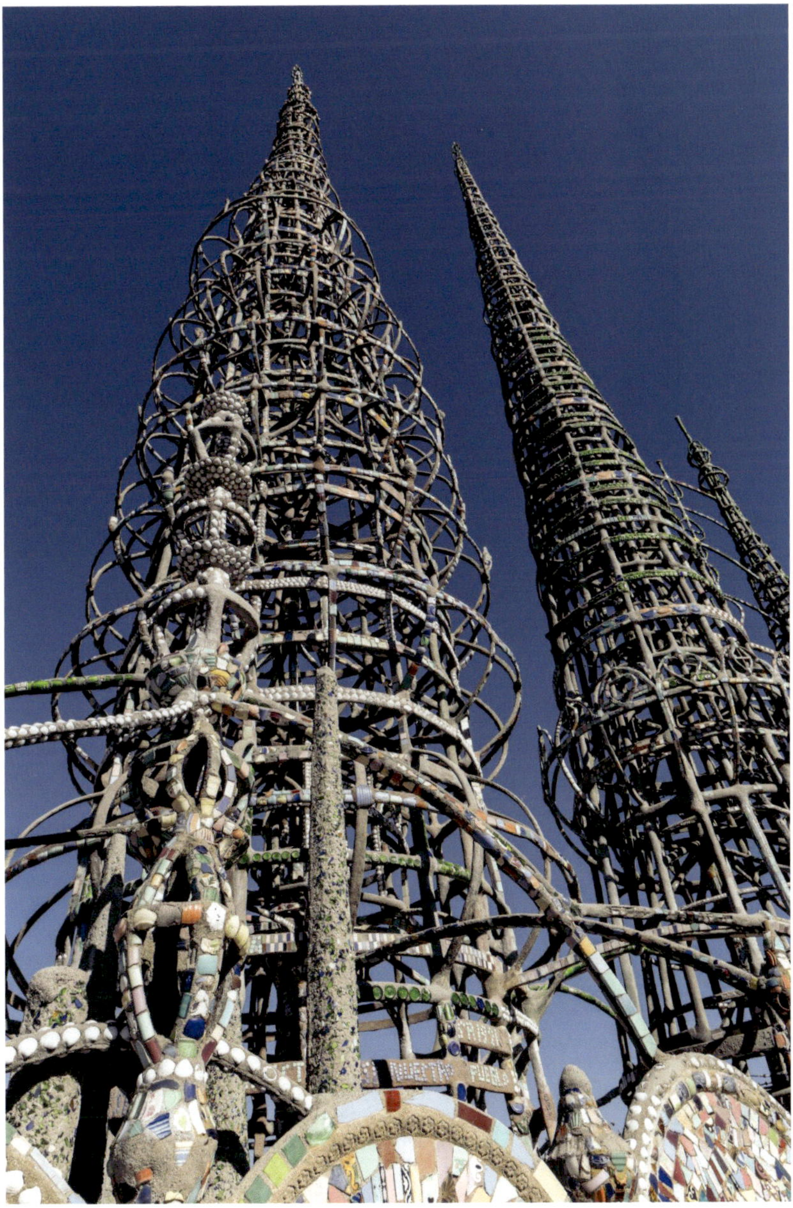

Figure 5. Watts Tower. Public domain.

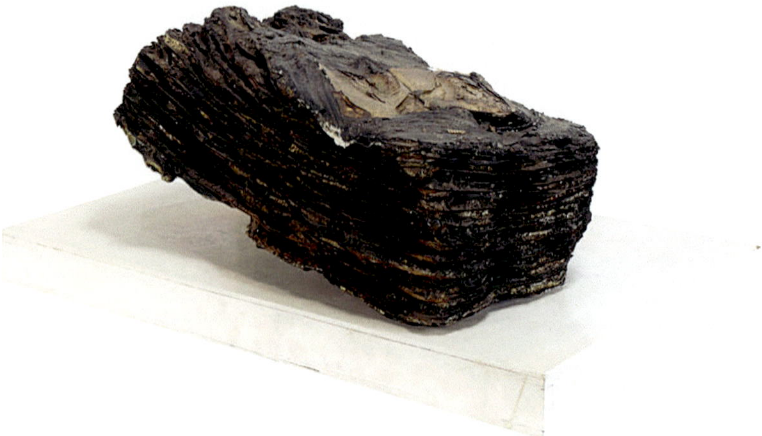

Figure 6. Noah Purifoy. *Watts Uprising Remains*, c. 1965–66. Round object assemblage. 24 x 24 x 6 in. (61 x 61 x 15.2 cm). Collection of Charles Britton.

and the Caribbean in particular. In his 1950 book *Discourse on Colonialism*, Césaire argued this about the alienations that came with colonialism: "Between colonizer and colonized there is room only for forced labor, intimidation, pressure, the police, taxation, theft, rape, compulsory crops, contempt, mistrust, arrogance, self-complacency, swinishness, brainless elites, degraded masses."[30] For Césaire, colonization alienated both colonizer and colonized from their best natures. It degraded both the colonizers and colonized as social beings and debased the colonized as ethical ones. Césaire said, for instance, "No human contact, but relations of domination and submission which turn the colonizing man into a classroom monitor, an army sergeant, a prison guard, a slave driver, and the indigenous man into an instrument of production."[31]

Black radical thinkers of the period like Hansberry and Césaire were trying to address the specific alienations that applied to Black workers, in general, and Black peoples, in particular. For them the alienations of racial segregation, colonialism, and labor exploitation had produced a social and ethical crisis like none other in the history of modern civilization. As Césaire stated, "*I* am talking about societies drained of their essence, cultures trampled underfoot, institutions undermined, lands confiscated, religions smashed, magnificent artistic creations destroyed, extraordinary *possibilities* wiped out."

The Watts rebellion bore witness to this phenomenon, that the value of a people and a community was diminished as white-owned property was protected, enhanced, and mourned. The people who took part in the rebellion were contesting a world that fulfilled property but not them. Hence, several of them seized that property to turn it into something else. Here was the chance to confer a new life on the objects that—up until that point—signified their estrangement from the world and its promises. Maybe by turning the property into art, they could liberate it from its established dictates and alienations. Maybe through art they could produce a world that felt like theirs. This experiment would yield the exhibition known as *66 Signs of Neon*.

66 Signs of Neon and the Poetics of a Neighborhood

"While the debris was still smoldering, we ventured into the rubble like other junkers of the community, digging and searching," Purifoy said, "but unlike others, obsessed without quite knowing why. . . . [W]e had collected three tons of charred wood and fire-molded debris. . . . [W]e gave much thought to the oddity of our found things . . . and what to do with the junk we had collected,"[32] he continued, this time identifying the aesthetic aspects of their venture. Believing that there was something worth finding, he said, "Things had calmed down, and so we took our wagon to the streets and looked for things that looked beautiful: the signs of neon, the signs that had melted and broken and pieces that were infused with glass. They looked like beautiful jewels in the sunshine."[33] With the neon signs and the other bits of ruin (some mangled pieces of charred steel and a scorched bible opened to the Epistles of Paul), they built an art exhibit that was first shown at Markham Junior High School in Watts and would then travel to eight US universities, finally stopping at the Washington Gallery of Modern Art.

One of the first pieces that was made for the exhibit was a sculpture that Purifoy named *Breath of Fresh Air*. The piece also served as the cover image for the exhibition booklet. It's composed of two stovepipes, standing at about 36 inches. Part of a tar paper roof is placed on top of it with a brace to hold the roof up. The pipes themselves are placed on a pedestal.[34]

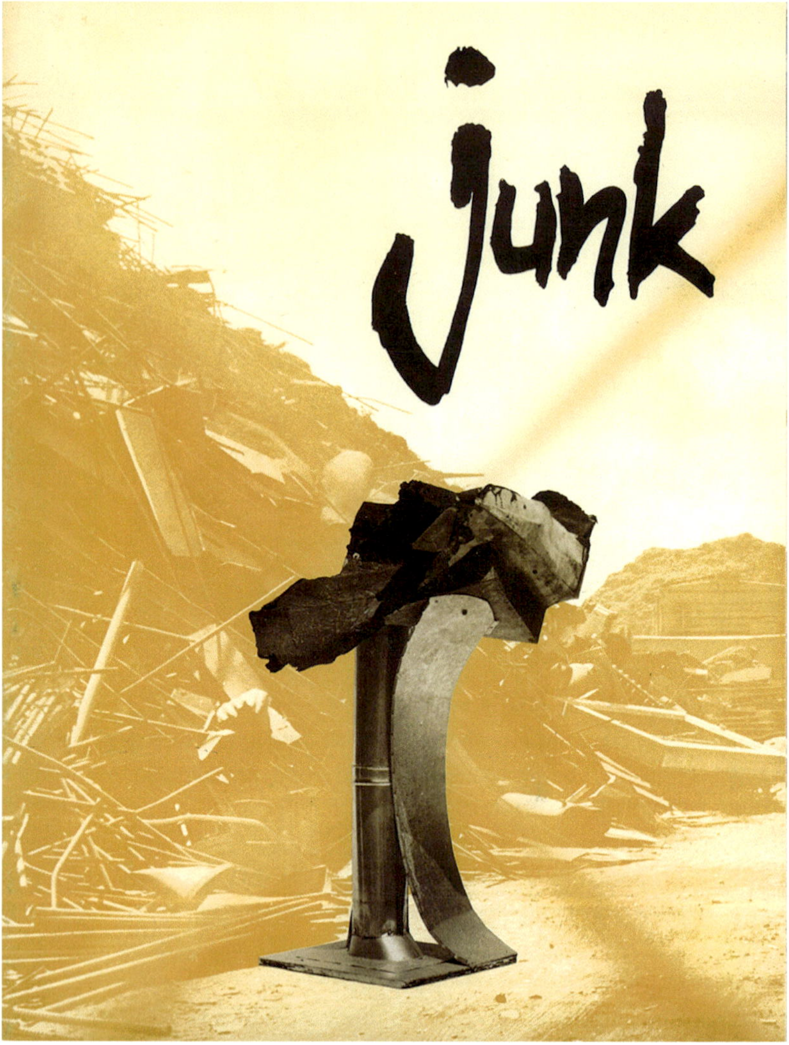

Figure 7. Noah Purifoy, *Breath of Fresh Air*. 1966. Reprinted with permission.

The sculpture's materials and its title have much to say about Watts, the rebellion, and the discourses that surrounded it. To begin with, its pedestal invokes and plays with the histories and features of canonical Western art. In ancient Greek and Roman art and architecture, pedestals were used to showcase statues of gods and heroes and to display treasured urns, porcelains, and sculptures.[35] In our modern era, designers have used them to add depth to an awkward looking space, to give viewers something to look at, to make a space appear larger, and to bridge different aesthetic styles. *Breath of Fresh Air* does all of this but at an angle.

Through its use of stove pipes from the neighborhood, the sculpture's pedestal elevates Watts—its residents and their homes—to a new status, one worthy of artistic observance and dignity. By doing so, the piece revises the all-too-common perception of Watts as a derelict and doomed part of the city. Instead, the sculpture gestures toward the homes and the lives that were cultivated there, giving them a depth and texture that was often denied them. The pedestal bridges two—seemingly incommensurate—worlds as well, the world of art and the world of a Black urban neighborhood. In this respect, the sculpture suggests that affiliations and associations can take place even between esoteric domains like art and the much maligned and misunderstood worlds of poor and working-class Black people. In addition, the stovepipes can be read as metaphors for the creations produced while the smoke is still clearing, implying that the exhibition itself was akin to the making of food for a people in need of sustenance. Set in the shadow of the McCone Report and its construction of the neighborhood as a social problem rather than a struggling community filled with rich possibilities that are simply in need of activation, the piece stands as a rebuttal to that document.

The title as well implies that the kind of artistic treatment and engagement with the neighborhood that the exhibition offered grants a breath of fresh air to a community enveloped by the pathologizing rhetoric of racism. As the fire helped to bring about this new breath, the piece also implies that the rebellion helped to give the neighborhood a new sense of self. We might say that the sculpture connotes a new name for the neighborhood in the rebellion's wake.

Breath of Fresh Air is the quintessence of assemblage. The curator and art critic William C. Seitz defined that art form by saying, "Assemblage is poetic rather than realistic, for each constituent element can be transformed. Physical materials and their auras are transformed into a new amalgam that both transcends and includes its parts."[36] In Purifoy's sculpture, the stovepipes, the roof, and the brace highlight how their everyday uses were part of the artfulness that people were delivering to life in the neighborhood. It is important to note, however, that the everyday uses of the pipe, the roof, and the brace are not incidental to that change. Their previous associations with the mundane and the domestic become the basis of an overturning. As Seitz argued, assemblage was an art form in which "the accepted hierarchy of categories (as the surrealists delighted in pointing out) is disrupted."[37] Elaborating on the poetic nature of this art practice, he said, "When the meanings of highly charged units impinge on a poetic as well as on a physical or visual level, significant expression becomes possible."[38] *Breath of Fresh Air* takes the charged meanings of the neighborhood and reformulates them so that the neighborhood is re-seen as an amalgam of artistic and poetic alternatives, alternatives arising from the presumably mundane and the taken-for-granted.

Like the project on 107th Street, *66 Signs of Neon* was trying to produce a poetic rendering of the neighborhood, one that would liberate the neighborhood from the tired and dominant frameworks imposed upon it. Discussing assemblage in relation to Black artists and Black neighborhoods in Los Angeles, the historian Daniel Widener writes, "Assemblages transformed the familiar, forcing new looks at old objects. In a neighborhood surrounded by junkyards and plagued by infrequent garbage collection, junk art asked the community to reexamine the true value of the objects around it."[39] Talking about the arts education program at the Center, Purifoy said, for instance, "Oftentimes, we'd take the children on trips to pick out objects—junk and etc.—and bring it back to the towers, to the art center, to do assemblages and collages and so forth. . . . We learned that it was rather natural and instinctive for the kids to assemble and disassemble an object, with the idea of counting the parts and so forth."[40] Hence, assemblage art proved to be a fitting method for children and for Black poor and working-class people since it appealed to the fundamentals of learning and was designed to disrupt accepted hierarchies and open new forms of expression. Connecting this aspect of the art form to the installation, Purifoy said, "The art works of 66 should be looked at not as particular things in themselves, but for the sake of establishing conversation and communication, involvement in the act of living."[41]

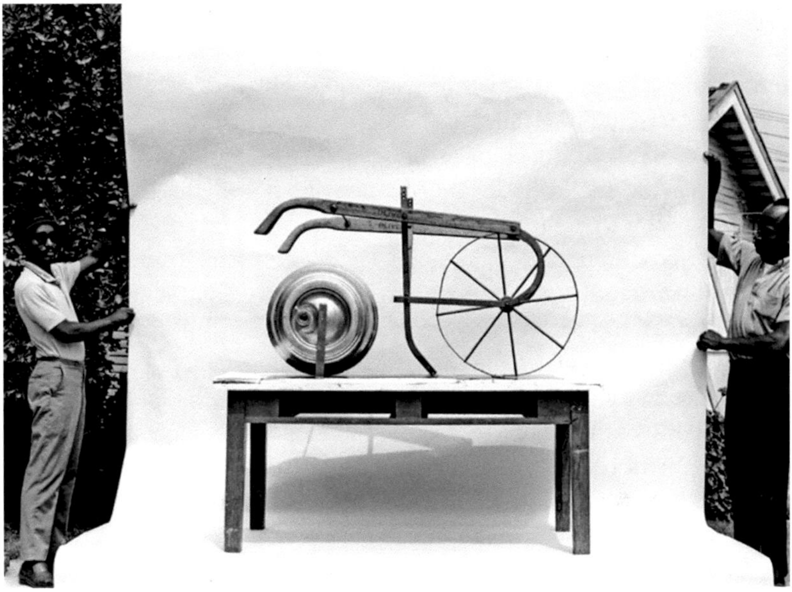

Figure 8. Darcy Robinson and Judson Powell with Noah Purifoy's *Barrel and Plow*. 1966. Photo by Harry Drinkwater.

Another piece that expresses the depths that reside in the taken for granted aspects of Black life is *Barrel and Plow*. Purifoy and Powell created it, and like *Breath of Fresh of Air* it too illustrates the sense of artfulness that people were bringing to their lives. To construct the piece, the artists mounted a beer barrel and a high wheel plow on a table. They placed the barrel in between the handles of the plow, where the farmer would stand.

There are many ways to read the piece. One way would be to place the work within the context of a community produced by Black migrants from the US South. As a result, the plow recalls the soil that those migrants tilled before reaching the West coast. Touching on that history, the McCone Report argued, "The First World War brought new immigrants into Los Angeles to fill the jobs opened by new industries. Some of these immigrants were Negroes from southern states, and they too settled in Watts."[42] Placing the barrel where a Black worker might have stood signifies the fact that the worker was producing commodities like the beer that were never meant primarily for the worker's enjoyment. Part of what alienated Black laborers was their inability to claim the pleasures of the things that they made. So even with the beer barrel's typical associations with alcoholism and overindulgence, it could also stand as the sign of the Black worker's chance at leisure and pleasure. Touching on how capitalism attempted to alienate the worker from the presumed "luxuries" of life, Marx argued that the "innermost soul of English capitalism" was both to force down workers' wages and to see their consumption of "brandy, gin, tea, sugar, foreign fruit, strong beer, printed linens, snuff, [and] tobacco" as unnecessary for production.[43]

As a sign of the people's commitment to deriving pleasure even from a life filled with alienation, the beer barrel can be interpreted as the will to keep labor and pleasure together. This reading of *Barrel and Plow*—as a work that insists that life be lived even in the midst of alienation—coheres with arguments made by Black diasporic artists and intellectuals of the time. For instance, in a 1962 letter to his nephew, James Baldwin wrote that part of the alienation mandated by whiteness is a rejection of sensuality. In the letter, he invoked the joyful freedom achieved by the folks of the neighborhood—the "pimps, whores, racketeers, church members and children—bound together by the nature of [their] oppression, the specific and particular complex risks [they] had to run," the ones who "ate and drank and talked and laughed and danced and forgot all about 'the man.'" He offered this definition of sensuality to his nephew: "To be sensual, I think, is to respect and rejoice in the force of life, of life itself, and to present that in all that one does, from effort of loving to the breaking of bread."[44] By reading *Barrel and Plow* alongside Baldwin's insistence on sensuality, we come away with a sense of the Black radical tradition as not simply exposing inequality but evolving forms of joy and pleasure as part of our birthright and our obligation.

Confronting inequality *and* rejoicing in the force of life was part of how many Black intellectuals and artists from the nineteenth century onward understood the meaning of culture. For instance, the *Presence Africaine* editors argued, "Culture is merely the vital effort through which each race and each individual by their experience and aspirations, their work and reflections, reconstruct a world which is filled with life, thought and passion and seems to thirst more than ever for justice, love, and peace."[45] Culture was, hence, not some inert thing waiting to be observed. It was the process and passion by which people involved themselves—to use Purifoy's words—in "the act of living." Black culture is what encouraged Black people to make their lives into artful dialogues with their historical and material conditions.

Aesthetics and Politics and the Shit That Needs Remodeling

For Purifoy, assemblage art would represent the attempt to achieve revelations about the self and the social world. In an artist statement from 1997, he said, "When the creative process is seen as a discipline it is applicable to any other discipline. . . . One does not have to be a visual artist to utilize their creative potential. Creativity can be an act of living a way of life, and a formula for doing the right thing."[46] Discussing further how art is simply one option for expressing creative potential, he went on to argue, "Within [each person] there's a creative process going on all the time, and it's merely expressed in an object called art. One's life should also encompass the creative process. We were trying to experiment with how you do that, how you tie the art process in with existence."[47]

For John Dewey, the aesthetic was also applicable beyond the terrain of art. He argued, "Every [aesthetic] experience is the result of interaction between a live creature and some aspect of the world in which he lives."[48] This interaction between human beings and the world describes politics as well. Aristotle, for instance, offered politics and art as social practices organized around "contriving and considering how something may come into being." In the *Nicomachean Ethics*, he said,

> Every art is concerned with bringing something into being, and the practice of an art is the study of how to bring into being something that is capable either of being or of not being, and the cause of which is the producer and not in the product. For it is not with the things that are or come to be *of necessity* that art is concerned, nor with the natural objects (because these have their origin within themselves).[49]

Art and politics unite in the disposition to make and remake. For Black radical traditions, the notion of culture represents this understanding, that we are not simply destined to the already given, that an alternative is possible, and that the materials for the alternative are already at hand.

Hence, the art that was produced from the rebellion referred to the riots as part of the people's efforts to refuse the world that was given them, to imagine an alternative to that world's alienations, and to use the warped, scorched, and discarded materials of that world to remake it. In this way, the people's art was a means of seeing the neighborhood and the rebellion anew, in ways that eschewed the pathologizing outlooks of the McCone report. In these alternative modes of seeing, we can catch a glimpse of the Black radical tradition's encouragement to reconceptualize Black communities and peoples as historical agents who can and must meet the pain of the world with a radical joy and creativity. As it was imprinted by that tradition, the art of the neighborhood was the mode of an alternative production of not only what the neighborhood was but what it could be.

Given that the task was to remake a world that was broken and warped even before the fires began, it is fitting that assemblage art would be the specific genre for the neighborhood's reinterpretation and renewal. The fractured and twisted objects that came from the rebellion were simply

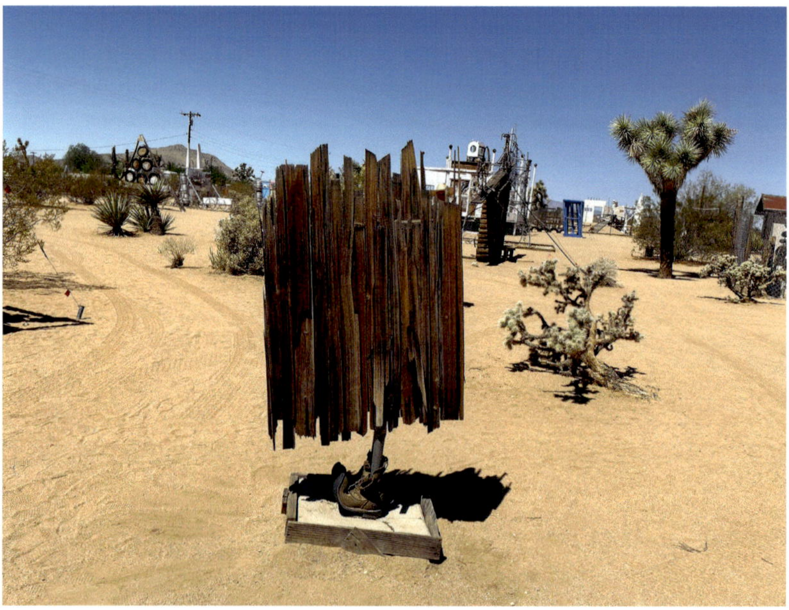

Figure 9. Desert Art Museum.

metaphors for a world that was already alienated because of poverty and race. Making use of the vestiges of alienation was the principal objective of the neighborhood's assemblage artists, a way of insisting that reshaping the world involves converting and rearticulating alienation into something else, a means of engaging the alienated world as a resource that is immediately eligible for re-creation. Understanding the immediacy of that resource and how assemblage art awakens our appreciation for it, Purifoy said, "Junk art, assemblage art . . . it's as close to human existence because it's all the castoffs we are utilizing here"[50] For Purifoy, how we handle junk is the basis of how we engage society's others and outcasts. If we have the imagination to see that a scorched Bible still has purpose, maybe we can see the worth of a despised people as well. Noting the possible relationship between assemblage and life, he would go on to say, "So I won't say that assemblage art is much like life itself, but it's closer to existence than any other art form. Because it's your shit that we're remodeling . . . and you got rid of it. And I come along and pick it up."[51]

2

Civilizing Missions and *The Hampton Project*

Carrie Mae Weems

There came a time when the artist Carrie Mae Weems got tired of the usual. "I just couldn't take it," she declared. "I just didn't want to make one more 16 x 20 black-and-white photograph that was matted with the black frame around it. I needed a larger format for expressing certain kinds of ideas and a certain kind of work."[1] Her installation *The Hampton Project* is one result of that exasperation. In it, Weems took pictures from storied Hampton University and printed them on sheer cloths that hung like banners from the ceiling. The pictures were from the school's photographic archive of African American and Native American students, photographs that the white woman photographer Frances Benjamin Johnston took for the Paris Exposition of 1900, photographs that would prove to the world that the school could civilize presumably savage peoples.

Talking about the school's collection of photographs and objects, Weems says, "[Hampton] has a tremendous archive that includes thousands of photographs—many of Indians on the central plains—along with a rather impressive collection of tribal artifacts, including a number of student donations; and several Hampton students became missionaries, both in Africa and on Indian lands, returning among their people to work, to convert."[2] In addition to being the treasured items of a university's history, the holdings can also be understood as the records of a racial and colonial project.

The preceding chapter showed how the McCone report constructed Black people who came from the South as unfit socially and morally for the modern world. The report also said that this unfitness was one of the reasons that the Watts Rebellion took place, but as we will see in this chapter, the South was a historic hotbed of civilizing projects, not only for Blacks but for Native Americans as well. The preceding chapter also looked at how a marginalized community was dismissed because of its racial makeup and its poverty. This chapter examines two groups of students who were dubiously embraced because of their potential to be remade as "proper" American men and women, a potential that was presumably undermined by their identities as Black and Native peoples. And like all civilizing projects, the one at Hampton claimed benevolence, but it proved to be a much more complicated affair than it seemed.

The Hampton Project illustrates how an HBCU—a historically Black college and university—was used as an experiment that would advance Americanization and settler colonialism. As both a civilizing and moralizing campaign, the school's educational system purported to lift Blacks and Native Americans out of backwardness and savagery and into the realms of segregated citizenship. This agenda was also a way of asserting control over Black and Indigenous peoples—over their bodies, families, and intimate lives, making the Hampton agenda part of the United States' larger racial and settler-colonial endeavor.

Capturing the significance of Weems's work, the art historian Sarah Elizabeth Lewis argues, "What emerged was a practice defined by an aesthetics of reckoning, works designed to force a confrontation with the unspeakable, allied to those who had been forgotten, unnamed, unheralded, and marshaled to examine the subjective construction of beauty and the biased formation of the 'history of power.'"[3]

The Hampton Project reckons with the unspeakable, allies with the overlooked, and sings a sorrow song for much more than what we usually assume the songs' laments to be. More than the matter of African American racial and class exploitation, *The Hampton Project* is also a moan about the imposition of what it means to be good and proper and about how those meanings were drawn against Black and Native peoples. Not simply focused on the exploitations of African Americans, the dirge that the installation offers bewails the breadth of US dominance. Hence, the cry of the sorrow songs applies to the circumstances of slavery and to the conditions of settler colonialism. Here, the line of a spiritual can be heard, one that pertains to the systems of power that affected Blacks and Native Americans alike: "I'm a rolling, I'm a rolling, Lord, I'm a rolling through this unfriendly world."

A Man Named Armstrong

After Weems mounted the installation, the university's officials objected to how she represented the photos from the archive. Using them to illustrate the assimilationist and civilizing aims of the school, she argued, "Education is conformity."[4] For Jeanne Zeidler, the then director of the Hampton University Museum, this robbed the graduates of their agency. The graduates did not conform to stereotypes. They transcended them, becoming missionaries, teachers, and doctors. But the installation does not deny that the students had agency. Indeed, the before and after photographs testify that they overcame great odds. Weems's installation suggests instead that even their agency as students, graduates, and professionals was imprinted by histories of race and settler colonialism. Their achievements while at Hampton and beyond were not the evidence of having transcended power but having been immersed in it.

Such an immersion was the founder's vision. In fact, he wanted students whose talents as leaders would arise from being in thrall to the school's momentous agendas. Skilled through power *and* captured by it—this was what it meant to be a Hampton student. Weems was not lost to this aspect of the school. "[From] the very beginning," she said about her work in general, "I've been interested in the idea of power and the consequences of power."[5]

To understand Hampton as part of the story of racial and colonial power, we must begin with General Samuel Chapman Armstrong. One of Weems's banners contains a photo of the Armstrong family (see figure 10). Four adults—one older man and three women—are seated. A child sits on the elderly man's lap. Another child stands between two of the women. Standing behind and over all of them is Samuel Chapman Armstrong. In the photo, Armstrong appears as the apex of a triangle with the family as his base. Weems has selected these words as the banner's epigraph: "With your missionary might you extend the hand of grace reaching down and snatching me up and out of myself."

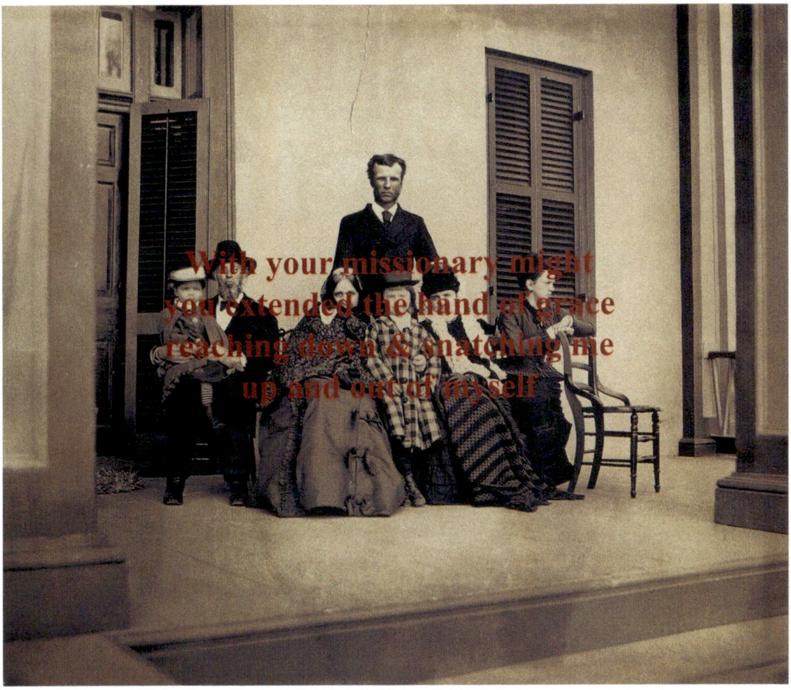

Figure 10. Carrie Mae Weems, *Armstrong Triptych* (center panel), from The Hampton Project. Ink on canvas. 103 x 120 x 1 in. Reprinted with permission.

Through this image, Weems conveys that Armstrong's educational project was in fact a generational one and that the legacies of settler colonialism and racism would be passed from one generation to another. By way of biography, Armstrong was a general for the Union Army, but before that he was the child of Richard Armstrong, a missionary for the American Board of Commissioners for Foreign Missions and an adviser to King Kamehameha III of Hawaii. About the Hawaiians, the elder Armstrong said: "This is a lazy people, and if they are ever to be made industrious the work must begin with the young. So I am making strenuous efforts to have some sort of manual labor connected with every school. . . . Without industry they cannot be moral." Clarissa Armstrong's opinions about Native Hawaiians would more than match her husband's. "Week after week passes," she decried, "and we see none but naked, filthy, wicked heathens with souls as dark as the tabernacles which they inhabit. The darkness of the people seems to destroy the beauty of the scenery around us."[6]

Discussing Richard Armstrong's vision for Native Hawaiians, the historian Gary Okihiro writes, "As chief administrator he was charged with oversight of 'private and public morals' in some two hundred schools then in operation." Believing that education and land utilization were defining problems for the kingdom, the senior Armstrong's curriculum "stressed agriculture ('proper' land use) for boys and homemaking (preparation for motherhood) for girls." And so began the moral agendas of manual education in Hawaii.

Right after his father died, Samuel Chapman Armstrong would leave Hawaii in 1860 to attend Williams College in northwestern Massachusetts. In those days, the school was known as a "mecca for missionaries' sons."[7] In fact, the founder of the American Board of Commissioners for Foreign Missions Samuel Mills, was a Williams alumnus, who attended the college in 1806. After meeting a young Hawaiian named Henry Obookiah, Mills would found a school for "heathen youth" in Cornwall, Connecticut. By the time Armstrong became a student there, colonialism in Hawaii had become part of the school's lore and reputation.

Taking inspiration from his father's vision, Samuel would devise plans for Hampton. As he said, "It meant something to the Hampton School, and perhaps to the ex-slaves of America, that, from 1820 to 1860, the distinctly missionary period, there was worked out in the Hawaiian Islands, the problem of the emancipation, enfranchisement and Christian civilization of a dark-skinned Polynesian people in many respects like the Negro race."[8] For Armstrong, one presumably successful experiment with a "dark-skinned people" could be applied to the circumstances of another. As a result, he would make Hampton into a laboratory, one that would use the rigors of manual labor to solve the problem of acculturating African Americans initially and Native Americans subsequently, socializing them into the norms (and hierarchies) of US society.

The banner associates the family with the Armstrongs' agenda for the school. Just as Armstrong stands as lord of the people in the photo, he would also stand as patriarch of the young people in the school. As the family members are carefully arranged horizontally beneath him, the students would be turned into a perfectly constructed line. The banner suggests that family would become the transmitter of racial and colonial power. In terms of the Armstrongs, Richard would beget that power through manual education in Hawaii, and Samuel would father it through the curriculum at Hampton.

When Armstrong arrived at Hampton in 1866, he was appointed to supervise nine counties in Virginia by General Oliver Otis Howard, who was then commissioner of the Bureau of Refugees, Freedmen and Abandoned Lands (popularly known as The Freedman's Bureau) and who would become the subsequent founder of Howard University. Two months after his arrival, Armstrong wrote the American Missionary Association (AMA), which had already established eight schools for newly freed Blacks from 1867 to 1868, telling them of his interest in building his own school that would

> prepare colored teachers for southern schools; teachers who will cost much less than whites; who can live the year through in one place, thus saving expense of transportation; who, in fact, can make a living out of their schools, and after being started, support themselves [through augmenting their low salaries with money earned through manual skills learned at school].[9]

Armstrong dreamed of a school that would train Black teachers and dispatch them as cheap laborers. Those alumni would socialize other Blacks—through word and deed—into an accommodationist gospel.

Even though the school tried to bring the Black and Native students as close to that ideal as possible, Armstrong never believed that they were capable of truly attaining that ideal. Their presumed inability to do so was for him even an advantage. One of the benefits of having Black women teachers, he said, would be that they could "penetrate the country and singly, occupy isolated and remote places where our [Northern white] ladies could never go."[10] While white women might have their virtue and gender violated in rural and remote places, there would be no such transgression for Black teachers, especially the women among them. Slavery and its laws had already established that there was no such thing as a virtuous Black woman, and no infraction in the countryside could strip them of a dignity that they never possessed in the first place. Their existence outside the norms of true womanhood would account for both the "freedom" of Black women's movement and the cheapness of their labor. The image on Weems's banner conveys an ideal of family, respectability, and gender normativity. It was meant to be an example that the school's students would constantly reach for but one that would always remain out of their grasp.

But Armstrong's plan of labor exploitation was vital to a much larger agenda. The historian James Anderson notes, for instance, "In Armstrong's view, northern capital and cheap black labor was critical to southern economic reconstruction and reunion with the Northeast."[11] In 1875, Armstrong declared, "The Eastern states have the capital and experience . . . while the South has the cheap labor; to bring the two together is to cement a real peace between the sections."[12] Northern capital would recoil from Black labor demanding its rights. As far as people like Armstrong were concerned, attracting Northern capital was necessary to restore the South. A principal way of achieving that was by producing a trained but docile Black middle class. With this vision, "peace" between the North and the South would come by permitting slavery's devaluations of Black labor to taint emancipation.

Extending bondage into freedom also meant undermining the political rights that Blacks won after the Civil War. Anderson states, for instance, "Armstrong instructed black leaders to 'stay out of politics because they were not capable of self-government,' and he blamed the black voters for creating situations in which 'no white race on this earth ought to endure or will endure.'"[13] Moreover, Armstrong argued, "'The votes of Negroes have enabled some of the worst men who ever figured in American politics to hold high places of honor and trust.'"[14]

But such claims were challenged throughout. Contrary to arguments that Reconstruction was a time of political and social mayhem, W. E. B. Du Bois argued in *Black Reconstruction in America*, "By 1865, there was strong testimony to the efficiency of the Negro worker."[15] The white newspaper editor Whitelaw Reid, for instance, said, "Returning from St. Helena in 1865, Doctor Richard Fuller was asked what he thought of the experiment of free labor, as exhibited among his former slaves, and how it contrasted with the old order of things. 'I never saw St. Helena look so well,' was his instant reply; 'never saw as much land as there under cultivation—never saw the same general evidences of prosperity, and never saw Negroes themselves appearing so well or so contented.'"[16]

And about the building of educational institutions, Du Bois determined, "There can be no reasonable doubt that common school instruction in the South, in the modern sense of the term, was founded by the Freedmen's Bureau and the missionary societies, and that the state public school system was formed mainly by Negro Reconstruction governments."[17] Pointing to the role of formerly enslaved Blacks in that endeavor, Colonel Richard P. Hallowell added, "'The whites had always regarded the public school system of the North with contempt. The freedmen introduced and established it, and it stands today a living testimony.'"[18] Hence, despite Armstrong's claim that Black people were "'not capable of self-government,'" there was ample evidence that they were not only capable but exemplary.

Weems's banner presents the white bourgeois family as the household from which settler colonialism and racial dominance arose. In this regard, there was nothing exceptional about the Armstrongs. Colonialism and slavery had been family affairs long before Richard dreamed up manual education in Hawaii. Other families had devised ways to bend labor for profit. Passing their methods from one generation to the next, those families would ensure that racism and colonialism would never simply be matters of the past.

Armstrong's vision of Black labor was stamped with issues of gender, class, morality, and race. Complex arrangements like these are what Weems's work has always tried to capture. As she said, " The one thing that I've been disappointed about for many, many years is the way in which the work is always so deeply located, for writers, in race. That many of these other kinds of questions haven't been fully explored at all."[19] In *The Hampton Project*, we can see how she coaxes the viewer to see how multiple social factors come together and how art and Black radicalism can be turned into microscopes for viewing the details. Soon we'll discover how Armstrong's vision involved not only African Americans but Native Americans as well.

The Colonial Undercurrents of an HBCU

"Snatching me up and out of myself"—these words are particularly meaningful when viewing the installation's photos of Native American students. One of the banners includes an image of Adele Quinney of the Stockbridge-Munsee nation. She's seated in a chair, wearing a black Edwardian blouse. In Johnston's original photo, she described her as a "Girl, whose every physical measurement is artistically correct."[20] Another banner includes Johnston's photo of John Wizi, who is also sitting, wearing a tie and a Wallace and Barnes jacket. He's clean-shaven with a military-style haircut. In Johnston's photo, we are told that Wizi is "Sioux" and the "Son of Chief Wizi of Crow Creek, SD."[21] Weems offers the two photographs of Quinney and Wizi as examples of young people who have been "snatched" away from themselves and their families.

Referring to her research for *The Hampton Project*, Weems said, "Hampton University is unique for several reasons: it's the first educational institution in North America to offer programs of study to both African Americans and North American Indians."[22] Noting the ironies of this convergence, she also stated, "In 1868 its first students were freed slaves, and in 1878 its first Indian students were former hostages and prisoners of war—a fascinating contradiction."[23] As the school matriculated African Americans and Native Americans, it would reveal the similarities between emancipation and captivity.

On November 5, 1878, sixty-two Native American youths would arrive on the campus, prisoners from the Red River War in the Southern Plains. They were brought there from Fort Marion, Florida, by Richard Henry Pratt, a veteran officer in the Union Army and a serviceman in the Indian Wars on the frontier.[24] Fifteen of the young hostages would remain at Hampton, joined later by two more who had been held in New York state.[25] The rest would be taken west to tribal encampments. Those seventeen pupil-prisoners hailed from the Omaha, Cheyenne, Comanche, Arapaho, and Kiowa nations, but by the program's end in 1923, the school would have enrolled 1,300 Native students from sixty-five other nations.[26] Praising Hampton's system of industrial training, Pratt said that he was "unable to find any school so nearly meeting my views for Indian education."[27]

Discussing those early days, Armstrong said that he only intended to enroll Black students but a "Macedonian cry came from some Indian ex-prisoners of war in Florida."[28] In the Book of Acts, the apostle Luke tells the story of a night-time vision that the apostle Paul saw, one in which a Macedonian man beseeched him saying, "Come over into Macedonia and help us." And so he and his companions—Timothy and Silas—went into Macedonia, assured that the Lord had called them to preach the gospel to the people in that province.

According to Armstrong, the hostages at Fort Marion, had a similar plea as the man in Paul's dream. No longer willing to be "bad Indians" (as the schools that rejected Pratt's initial requests had called them), they would surrender themselves to Armstrong to be made into a less "peculiar people."[29] Presumably with spade, plow, hoe, awl, and hammer in hand, they would take their place alongside the Black students to build and walk along the "white man's road."[30]

But Armstrong contrived his Macedonian tale. In fact, a year before the child-captives came, he had proposed to the Secretary of the Interior Carl Schurz to enroll students from the Nez Perce tribe of the Pacific Northwest. The head of the Nez Perce nation, Chief Joseph, had maintained that his land was illegitimately claimed by the United States. He set out to reclaim the land peaceably, proposing to share it even with the white settlers. US officials, however, rebuffed both his claim and offer. Instead, they pursued him and his people ruthlessly after he was forced to defend his nation. The general who was tasked to convince the Nez Perce to leave their ancestral lands and settle on reservations was none other than General Oliver Otis Howard, Armstrong's former supervisor. Angered by Joseph's refusal, Howard warned him that "he must not complain if evil happened to him."[31] Making good on his threat, Howard murdered many of the Nez Perce's women and children.

Believing he could capitalize on this slaughter, Armstrong calculated that a captive people would be ripe for the civilizing agenda of an industrial school. But his presumptions that the Nez Perce needed civilizing bore a similar irony to his contention that Black people could not produce a functioning society. Throughout his efforts to preserve his people's territory, Joseph demonstrated a sophisticated understanding of democratic principles of cooperation and coexistence. "We only ask an even chance to live as other men live," he said. "Let me be a free man—free to travel, free to stop, free to work, free to trade where I choose, free to choose my own teachers, free to follow the religion of my fathers, free to think and talk and act for myself."[32] As Armstrong's interest in the Nez Perce and the young prisoners attests, Indigenous lands and children had become some of the most vital spoils of settler-colonial wars.

Those spoils are implied in *The Hampton Project*. To invoke Armstrong's civilizing project, for instance, Weems uses this 1875 photo by the Mormon photographer Charles Roscoe Savage (see figure 11). It's titled *Indian*

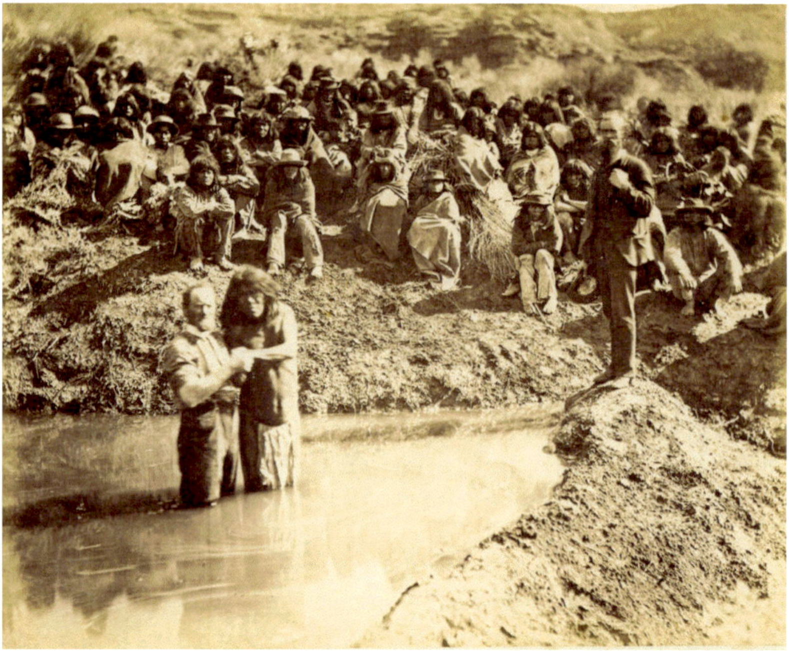

Figure 11. Charles Roscoe Savage. *Indian Baptism*.1875. Public domain.

Baptism, and it depicts two white men and a group of Paiute men. One white man, a Mormon leader by the name of Daniel P. McArthur, is in the water about to baptize a Native man. The other white man, Sheriff Augustus P. Hardy, is standing, fully suited.[33] Except for the Paiute man who is awaiting baptism, all the other Indigenous men are sitting down, and even the Native man who is standing is held up by McArthur, as if he is unused to moving upright.

Savage's photo presents the Native people as primate-like, while the white men are superior because of their erectness. The photo's message suggests that Christian conversion is part of their rise from savagery and that maybe one day they will be able to walk upright like the white men who are their betters. Almost its own version of a lost people's Macedonian cry, the photo implies that the men's indigence is due to culture rather than the devastation caused by continuous wars of colonialism. But in

Weems's rendition, the photo is observed as part of a colonial gallery, an artifact of Armstrong's race-making agenda.

Who knows why the men cowered. Perhaps they did so because they remembered the slaughter of their people at Circleville, Utah, in 1866. Just nine years before the picture was taken, Mormon settlers gathered some thirty Paiute persons into a church meetinghouse and killed everyone, except the youngest children. Those children they "adopted" into local families, effectively turning them into slaves. By the mid-nineteenth century, the thieving and enslaving of Native children had become a "vibrant business" in Utah, California, and other southwestern territories.[34]

It was not incidental that Savage was a landscape photographer. Savage's photo can be situated in that period in which landscape photography, according to the historian Martin Berger, was a way of clarifying and fostering white identity.[35] Through landscape photography, photographers could produce Indigenously held land as empty of human beings, generally, and Indigenous communities, particularly. The photos could spin a yarn that the lands within what is now the United States was always part of the United States and simply waiting for white (i.e., industrial) development. But Savage's photo includes what other landscape photographs denied—the presence of Native peoples. Hence, *Indian Baptism* exposes the colonial ideology that lies underneath landscape photography. By including the Savage photo in the installation, Weems points to how "civilizing" Indigenous peoples was a component in the drama of colonial land theft, a drama that was part of Hampton's history as well.

Savage's photograph, like all the others, is cast on muslin, a fabric that was spun from a rare species of cotton grown in a region that spanned West Bengal in India and Bangladesh. In the seventeenth and eighteenth centuries, the fabric was the subject of myths. It was said that this type of muslin was so delicate that if placed on the grass it could disappear into the morning dew. Known by such names as *evening dew* and *running water*, the fabric boasted of a whisper-like quality. It is fitting then that Weems would choose muslin as the material for such a delicate history as that of Hampton, one in which dreams of young people's education would be enmeshed with the history of the US empire. In hushed tones, the fabric passed on a subjugated knowledge.

Referring to a 1990 installation that Weems created about social movements around the world, the theorist bell hooks said about Weems, "As

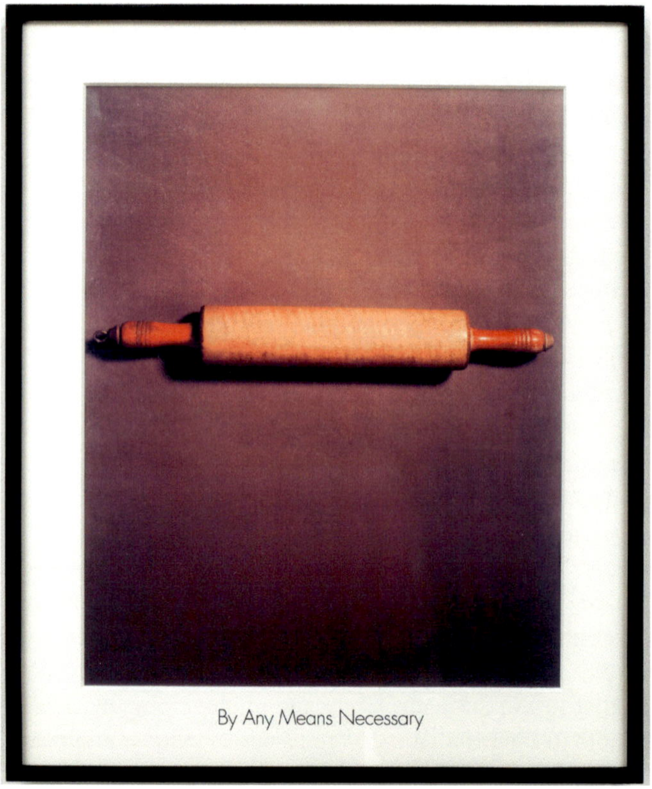

Figure 12. Carrie Mae Weems. *By Any Means Necessary*. From And 22 *Million Very Tired and Angry People* installation. 1989–1990. Polaroid. 24 x 20 in. Reprinted with permission.

[*And 22 Million Very Tired and Angry People*] makes clear, rage against injustice, as well as the weariness that comes with protracted struggle, is not the exclusive property of black people."[36] *The Hampton Project* shows how Native peoples had every right to inveigh against colonial oppression. It also makes clear that Black radicalism must acknowledge that fury. The installation, moreover, illustrates how confronting the painful elements within Black history is a vital gesture for Black freedom struggles. Indeed, *The Hampton Project*'s interest in how a celebrated school participated in the madness of empire demonstrates—in hooks's words—how Weems's art "visually engages a politics of anticolonialism."[37] In the next section, we'll see how interlacing a politics of anti-colonialism with traditions of Black freedom necessarily means interrogating gender and sexuality.

So That They Can Be Moral

The photography scholar Laura Wexler tells us that Frances Benjamin Johnston was hired by Hollis Burke Frissell, the second principal of Hampton Institute, as part of a "public relations assignment,"[38] one designed to promote the school's successes at the 1900 Paris Exposition. It would be the institution's chance to prove to the world that Blacks who had just been uplifted from slavery and Native peoples who had recently been subdued by war could be Americanized. The artist and historian Jeannene Pryzblyski speculates that the photographs "were meant to reassure an international community that the United States had its Negro problem firmly in hand."[39] But the photographs were also meant to convey that the United States could control Native insurgency as well. For both African Americans and Native Americans, imposing bourgeois norms of gender and sexuality was central to that control.

Weems includes two photos that Johnston took for the Paris Exposition. One photo, *The Old Folks at Home*, depicts an older Black couple, dining at a makeshift table in modest clothes. Their home has the earnest inadequacies of a humble dwelling. The table is not the standard height, giving the impression that the couple can only mimic domesticity but not achieve it. If we compare, *The Old Folks at Home* to *Indian Baptism*, we come away with the idea that Native American and African American destitution is the result of a shared primitivism, a failure to sufficiently enter modern culture.

Johnston's other photo is titled A *Hampton Graduate at Home* (see figure 14). In contrast to *Old Folks at Home*, this family is complete with husband, wife, and children sitting in a modern and spacious dining room set within a house with a staircase. The husband, wife, and three children are all clothed in the day's fashion. The photo illustrates Hampton's presumed power to create new types of people, ones who are brought up from their lowliness, moderns who can inhabit and symbolize the bourgeois and heteropatriarchal home.

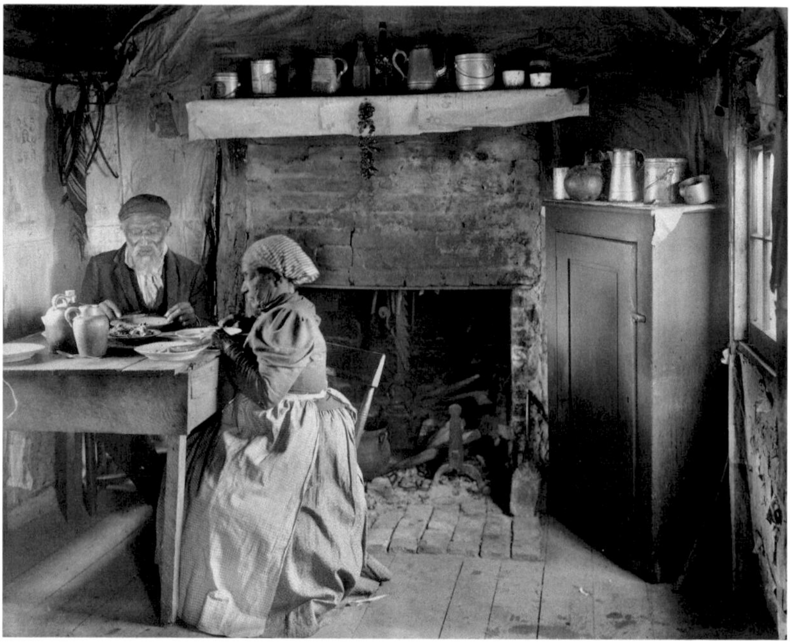

Figure 13. Frances Benjamin Johnston. *Old Folks at Home.* Museum of Modern Art, New York. Reprinted with permission.

Like *A Hampton Graduate at Home*, another photo, *Group Portrait in the Garden* (see figure 15), depicting Native American students at Hampton, suggests the school's final achievement—that is, Native men and women who are properly gendered and composed. Like the previous photo, this one testifies to the school's ability to upgrade the destitute. In the case of Native Americans, Armstrong believed that coeducation was especially beneficial for their uplift. In the school's efforts to make proper men and women out of the Indigenous students, the officials again pointed to the presumed successes among the African American students. Armstrong said, for example, "An experience of ten years in educating together negro adults of both sexes, many of them being of the poorest class, is evidence that the co-education of Indian youth will succeed."[40] According to the historian Donal F. Lindsey, Armstrong "contended the educated Indian

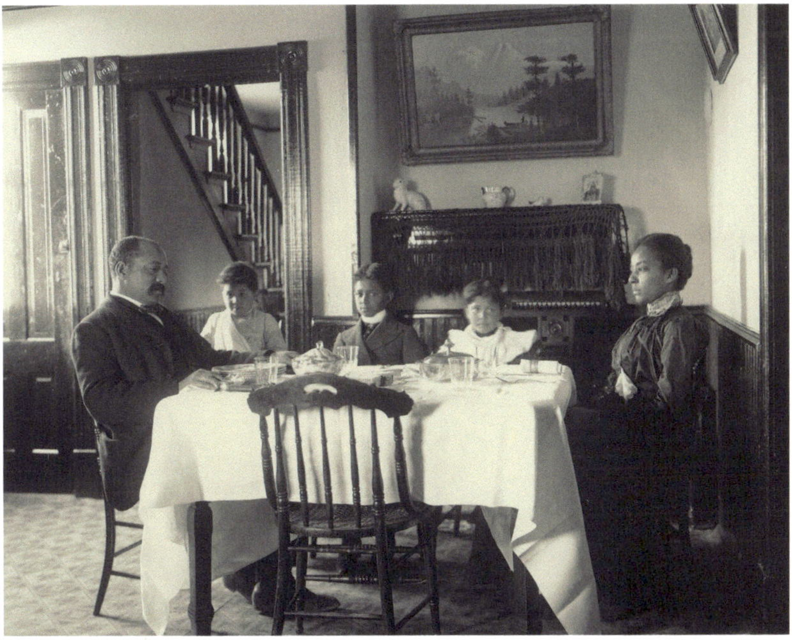

Figure 14. Frances Benjamin Johnston. *Hampton Graduate at Home*. Museum of Modern Art, New York. Reprinted with permission.

male would regress unless he found a mate to uphold his new values."[41] As Armstrong's remarks and the photos make clear, the civilizing mission for African Americans and Native Americans was not only raced but gendered and (hetero)sexualized as well.

Civilizing Native peoples, for Armstrong, required that they mimic—as best they could—white families like his. To this end, the women's Edwardian blouses signal their ladyhood as the men's military uniforms suggest the fabled masculinity of US empire. The Indigenous men's dress is, therefore, filled with a bitter irony: The children who were captured would be made to look like the ones who captured them.

The two photos also point to the fact that Armstrong and the Hampton staff often imagined African Americans and Native Americans as similarly uncivilized. In fact, Armstrong believed that he might win donations if he

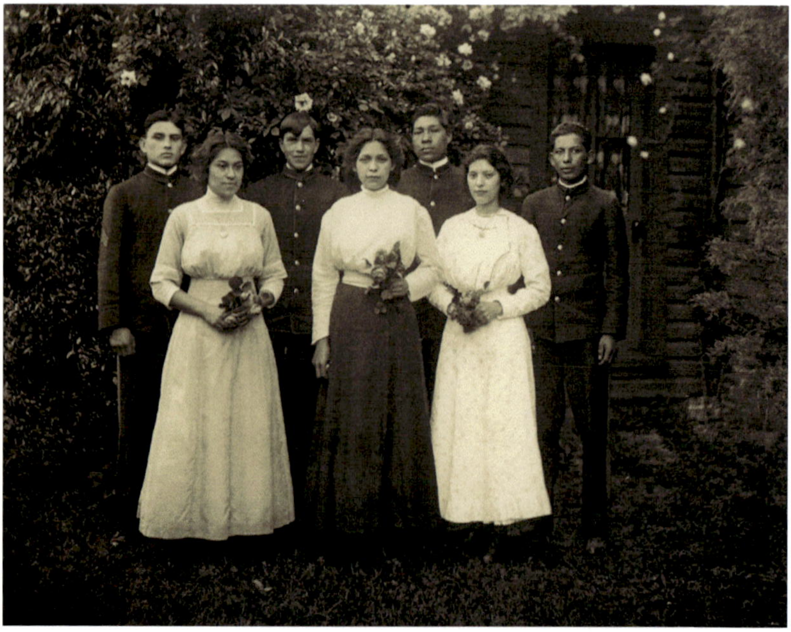

Figure 15. Carrie Mae Weems. *Untitled (Group Portrait in the Garden)*. From The Hampton Project. 2000. Ink on muslin. 71 x 93 in. Reprinted with permission.

constructed both Native students and African American students as barbarians in need of civilization. Hence, he wrote to his wife Emma, "I am on the track of some more money—it will be necessary to prove that the darky is an Indian in order to get it: but I can easily do that . . . Keep dark and send me your thoughts on the Indian and the darky—SAME THING, aren't they?"[42]

Like Armstrong, Pratt also believed that Blacks and Natives occupied the lowest rungs of civilization and could only be redeemed through white American culture. "The negro . . . is from as low a state of savagery as the Indian," he argued, "and in 200 years' association with the Anglo-Saxons he has lost his languages and gained theirs; has laid aside the characteristics of his former savage life, and to a great extent, adopted those of the most advanced and highest civilized nation in the world, and has thus become fitted as a fellow citizen among them."[43] As far as Pratt was concerned,

Black people's experience with American civilization boded well for Native Americans. He said, for instance, "Then, I argued, it is not fair to denounce the Indian as an incorrigible savage until he has had at least the equal privilege of association. If millions of black savages can become so transformed and assimilated . . . there is but ONE PLAIN DUTY RESTING UPON US with regard to the Indians, and that is to relieve them of their savagery and other alien qualities by the same methods used to relieve others."[44] Put another way, what the middle passage and slavery provided Black people as a matter of course could become—for the school's African American and Native American students—a matter of policy.

The banners depicting African American and Native American students and alumni produce a labyrinth of images and histories that many probably did not realize were connected. Because of the ways that the diaphanous banners are hung—staggered and overlapping, viewers experience the histories of Black slavery and emancipation, and Indigenous slaughter and conversion as braided rather than disconnected. Textiles have allowed contemporary artists to invoke memory and history,[45] and Weems uses muslin to summon the braided histories of African American racialization and Native American colonization.

It should come as no surprise that making African American and Native American students into bourgeois men and women would necessarily alienate the students from their families. Take, for example, the story of Anna Bender. She would become the first Chippewa woman to graduate from Hampton. She was reunited with her family after years at the Lincoln Institute in Philadelphia, a school she described as "the only home I can distinctly remember."[46] Writing of the day that she met her family in Minnesota, she told of how her mother bought her apples at a store near the train station to comfort her after she burst into tears from meeting her kin who were more like strangers. Describing her experiences that evening, she said, "As we gathered around the table later a great wave of homesickness came over me. I could not eat for the lump in my throat and presently put my head down and cried good and hard, while the children looked on in surprise."[47] The process that turned Bender into a proper lady would also make her reunion with her family into an estrangement.

Believing in Hampton's powers to educate supposed barbarians, President Rutherford B. Hayes declared before Congress that the school was "destined to become an important factor in the advancement of civilization among Indians."[48] The idea that a school can remake the people in it has its origins in the earliest theorizations of the modern academy. In *The Conflict of the Faculties*, for example, the philosopher Immanuel Kant theorized the modern Western university as an institution that could confer upon students a new kind of personhood. As he argued, the university is endowed "to admit . . . students seeking entrance . . . , to grant degrees or confer the universally recognized status of 'doctor' on free teachers (that is, teachers who are not members of the university) in other words to *create doctors*."[49] In this capacity, the university does not simply grant degrees, it makes qualitatively different kinds of people. As far as officials like Armstrong were concerned, industrial education would be a mechanism for creating new kinds of Black Americans and Native Americans. And as Weems's banners imply, the two groups would become siblings within a colonial and racial order that was distinctly American.

Freedom's Extension of Slavery and Colonialism

Another Johnston photo that Weems uses is titled *Trade School. Shoemaking*. A white-appearing instructor is seated at a small table with two Native American students. All three are aproned and assembling shoes. Two African American students are seated behind them and to the right. They are aproned and making shoes as well. Similarly clothed and to the right of the African American students sits another Indigenous student at a sewing machine. (See figure 16.) Printed on a fabric with its own associations with racialized and colonized labor, the photo not only exemplifies the school's curriculum but its investment in racialized labor conditions as well.

In an 1898 appeal for funds, Hampton's second principal H. B. Frissell was clear how important the students' labor power was to the school and to the nation. Regarding Native Americans, he said, "Twenty years ago, Capt. Pratt brought fifteen prisoners of war from Fort Marion, St. Augustine, to Hampton and remained there one year bringing in the meantime other Indians from the West. So successful was that first experiment in industrial education that Carlisle School was established and now hundreds of thousands of dollars, which were formally devoted to fighting the Indians, are given by the government to training their children in industrial schools."[50] Here, Frissell praises Pratt, who would become the founder and

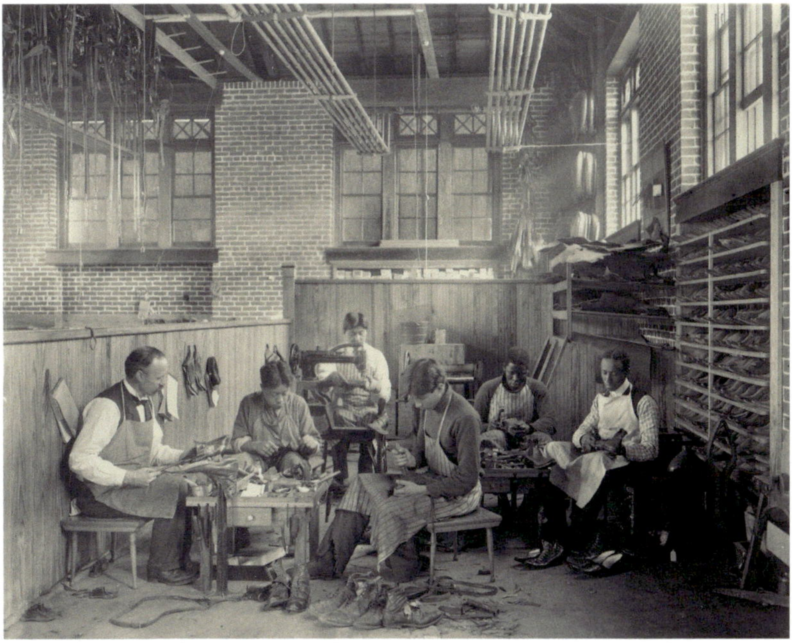

Figure 16. Frances Benjamin Johnston. *Trade School. Shoe-making*. Museum of Modern Art, New York. Reprinted with permission.

superintendent of the infamous Carlisle School. While there, Pratt would notoriously declare, "Kill the Indian in him, and save the man."[51] But just as startling is that Frissell's letter inadvertently acknowledges that industrial education was war by other means. Turning Native Americans into laborers for capital could be a quiet way of subduing them.

Discussing the ways that she approaches places and institutions, Weems says, "I'm usually interested in the little-known facts about a place. It's often the little-known facts and secrets that make a place/thing/person."[52] That the school was a factory for racialized and colonized labor was one of those secrets. Sixteen years before Frissell made his appeal to would-be donors, a November 11, 1882, article in the *Virginia Star* titled "Indian Labor" discussed the matriculation of Indian students at Hampton. After discussing the Native American and Black students who were contracted to make "2000 pairs of brogans"[53] and "seventy-five sets of double plow harnesses,"[54] the article quotes from authorities who say that the shoes and plows that the students made were "superior to any which could be produced by hand by three men in a hundred who can be found in Northern factories."[55]

According to the article, General Armstrong took this as a sign that Indigenous students could modernize, Americanize, and domesticate their communities. He said, "Those who have already gone back from those institutions are, as a rule, doing well, and prove not only that the Indian under favoring circumstances, is able and willing to work, but that he may be made a valuable producer and citizen at far less cost than it takes to fight him."[56] Armstrong's remarks reveal that for its primary architects, manual education was only incidentally motivated by academic ideals and mainly by economic and political ones.

For Hampton's founders, industrial education was also an experiment in extending certain contours of slavery after its legal abolition. In his letter, Frissell argued, for example, "Hampton has given an impetus to industrial education among the Negroes which is felt in every state of the South. But 75 per cent of the race still live in one-room cabins on rented land, in ignorance and poverty. Teachers of agriculture and home builders are needed."[57] For Frissell, the cure for this ignorance and poverty lay in the special way that industrial education could access a recent past. He said, "There is a danger that the blacks will lose the trades, which was their best heritage from slavery, unless industrial education is pushed. Well trained young women must go out to reconstruct the homes."[58] Industrial education would be a way of reuniting the North and the South by supplying Northern manufacturers with cheap labor in the South. Constituting that labor would mean educating Black Americans and Native Americans into a segmented and segregated workforce, one that reconstructed the "insights" of the plantation and the objectives of settler-colonial wars. For both groups of people, manual education would attempt to extend Black enslavement and Indigenous captivity into freedom's arena.

The positions that African Americans and Indigenous people occupied in the United States arose from the country's conjoined origins in slavery and settler colonialism. In the words of the Afro-Indigenous scholar Kyle T. Mays, the United States is "foundationally an anti-black and anti-Indigenous republic."[59] As he explains, "The introduction of African peoples as exploited people on Indigenous land set the stage for the exponential growth of capitalism."[60] For newly emancipated African Americans it meant imposing prior contours of servitude. For Native Americans, it involved moving them into the exploitable position of "free laborers" but only after colonizing their lands and murdering their people. These vicious moves would underwrite the so-called "freedoms" of capitalism.

Almost two thousand years ago when the ancient philosopher Pliny the Elder grumbled that too many of Rome's gold coins were being spent on Indian muslin, the rest of the city extolled the fabric by giving it names such as "woven wind" and "mist."[61] Long associated with trade, muslin in *The Hampton Project* can be read as an observance that the history of US capitalism is a fabric whose weaves are composed of race, indigeneity, and labor (see figure 17). Hanging the banners in the air, Weems seems to suggest that if we acknowledge the histories between and above us, we may be able to build a new partnership based on our entangled yesterdays. Zeroing in on this entanglement, she affixes a poem to one of the panels:

> Alpha, Omega, Delta, Psi
> I saw you
> become Hampton Alums
> the graduates of a stripped people
> echoes of your former selves
> hollowed relics
> of a former time
> I saw you
> Black and Indian co-mingle
> building the structure
> of your survival
> brick by brick
> with your own hands
> in your own time . . .

Part of what the Native American and African American students shared was the renewal of captivity through the achievement of education. But the banners also imply that in this lot they might find the resources for a coalition.

The Ensigns of a New Day

There's always a Black woman muse that shows up in Weems's work. As she says, "She's shown me a great deal about the world and about myself, and I'm grateful to her." "Carrying a tremendous burden," she observes, "she is a black woman leading me through the trauma of history. I think it's very important that as a black woman she's engaged with the world around her; she's engaged with history, she's engaged with looking, with being. She's a guide into circumstances seldom seen."[62]

A version of this Black woman came to Weems as she conceived *The Hampton Project*. Recalling this encounter, she said, "[A] very articulate female student said, 'You know, I walk through this campus often. I love this campus on the shore of the Chesapeake, but one day I noticed the street names, and I realized for the first time—truly realized—that they were Indian names; and it occurred to me that at one time Native Americans [helped build] this school so that I could go to school. And I think that's something that people should know. It's important.'"[63] The young woman identified how Indigenous people—along with African Americans—helped prepare a place for her and others. In doing so, the student complicated the notion of ancestors, suggesting that they are neither restricted by blood, heritage, or culture. The Native American students became the young woman's and other students' ancestors because of their labors.

After the African American historian and activist Vincent Harding moved to Denver, Colorado, with his family, he talked about how he was motivated to labor with the Indigenous and Chicanx inhabitants of the Southwest. He said, "We moved there in part because of the conviction that black people must assume major responsibility for the revisioning and reshaping of society. I felt intuitively that there were certain powers extant in the Southwest that I needed to be in touch with, among them the power of the natives of this land and the power of the Chicanos." Sensing that there could be a new type of communion, he went on to say, "And so part of my reason for going was to find a way to understand more fully and to participate more deeply in the life of native American and Chicago communities, and to see the ways in which children of Africa could come into a deeper relationship with children of Mexico and children of the earth."[64] For Harding a host of ancestors—natal and non-natal—called for a wiser engagement with the world and each other. These dead summon us to a new labor, one not governed by the terms of a capitalist order, a work not valued because of the brogans and plows that could be produced for that order.

Coming into a deeper relationship with one another necessarily means confronting and transcending legacies of anti-Black racism and settler colonialism. Clarifying what that relationship might look like, Harding wrote, "It was because I am convinced that the historian has a responsibility for the opening toward the future that I went to try to understand more fully these people, who I believe are not only openings in the past but also openings to the future and who can join in a conversation with the children of Africa and all other children of God who seek a new beginning for a society that badly needs one."[65] Harding suggests that by laboring for an alternative future we can reject the idea that we are doomed to a history filled with flesh-eating shackles and pox-ridden blankets.

Similarly, *The Hampton Project* implies that the artist has a responsibility akin to Harding's historian. As a matter of fact, we may look upon Weems's installation as much more than a peek into an unnerving past. It is also a doorway to a future of shared quests of freedom and autonomy, ones in which people will choose their own names, cultures, and gods.

Three years after arriving at Hampton and perhaps four years before seeing her family, Anna Bender—the Hampton student who broke down at her family's dinner table—wrote a short story about an Ojibwe boy named Quital who was saddened by the fact that his pony was too weak to have a chance at the Buffalo hunt while those of his friends were fast and strong. Seeing the boy's distress, his grandmother bade him to take the pony down to the creek and bring him back to her after washing him. Upon their return, she decorated the horse—as Bender wrote—"with bright colored Indian paints which she had made from some magic clay that she knew about."[66] So endowed, the horse and the boy beat all the other riders, allowing Quital to hunt more buffalo meat than all the rest. "These he took home to his grandmother," Bender wrote, "so that she had buffalo meat enough to last all the winter."[67] Writing after genocidal wars and the brutal separation of children from families, Bender suggests that Indigenous knowledge is both alive and needed after those tragedies. Thus, she and the other Native writers who were boarded provide sufficient proof that schools like Hampton and Carlisle did not in fact manage to murder the cultural identities of Native students.

We can also read some of the banners as signs that—contrary to Armstrong's and Pratt's intentions—the heart of ancestral cultures is still beating. At first blush, the portraits of Adele Quinney and John Wizi appear to fulfill the assimilationist's dream. But it is worth remembering that for artists textiles are ways of invoking tradition. So, while the young people may look completely Westernized, they rest on a medium with ancient associations.

The cultures of resistance and coalition suggested by *The Hampton Project* live in latter-day struggles as well. For instance, the 2016 protests around the Dakota Access Pipeline were originally organized by the young people of the Standing Rock tribe against a 1,172-mile underground oil pipeline that threatens their sacred lands and waters as well as those of other Indigenous nations. As the Lakota scholar and activist Nick Estes argues, "The protesters called themselves Water Protectors because they weren't simply against a pipeline; they also stood for something greater: the continuation of life on a planet ravaged by capitalism. This is reflected in the Lakota and Dakota philosophy of Mitakuye Oyasin, meaning 'all my relations' or 'we are all related.'"[68]

This philosophy of "all my relations" is a power that has gathered various peoples to its hallowed ground. In the words of Estes, "Black Lives Matter, Palestinian justice organizations, religious groups, military veterans, and many more from other social locations and movements galvanized support for the Indigenous-led resistance from far beyond the physical geography of the Standing Rock Indian Reservation."[69] As the protests were formed across communities of difference, they nodded to Harding's vision of a more profound and worldly communion. And if we read the protests in dialogue with *The Hampton Project*, we might say that the installation's ensigns heralded the kind of coalitions seen at Standing Rock.

When asked about the "ghostly" quality of *The Hampton Project*, Weems responded by saying, "[Perhaps] what you sense is the spirit of justice the work seeks. I fight for what I believe to be right; this is my spiritual challenge, always and in every way to embrace the breadth of our humanity, it's my duty to myself and the way that I am responsible to you; and this is so, even when it hurts."[70] For her the "spiritual" aspects of the installation

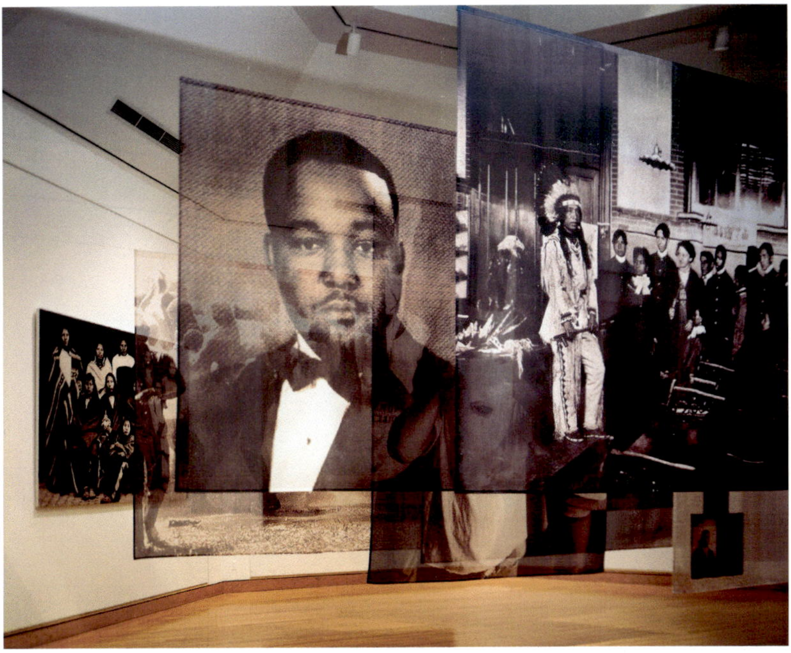

Figure 17. Carrie Mae Weems. *The Hampton Project*. 2000. Williams College Museum of Art. Photo by Arthur Evans. Reprinted with permission.

are anchored in a global quest for justice. And in freedom's journey, the dead still have their hope and being.

In the installation's cosmology, there is no unbridgeable gulf between the past and the present. Hundreds of years ago, people said that muslin was like "woven air." In fact, the banners suggest that the histories of race and colonialism have threaded their way into the present day and are waiting to be acknowledged and probed. In the banners' weaves, we can see that history is unavoidably crisscrossed. This sense of the intersecting quality of time accords with Estes's understanding of Native temporalities. He says, "Indigenous notions of time consider the present to be structured entirely by our past and by our ancestors. There is no separation between past and present, meaning that an alternative future is also determined by our understanding of our past. Our history is the future."[71]

Through muslin's long associations with whispers, the banners also speak softly about the politics of freedom. The work of liberation, the whispers say, means assuming responsibility for the unfinished freedom struggles of long ago. We might nominate muslin, then, as a fabric of Black radical traditions since—in Weems's hands—it invokes histories that are intricately entwined and barely visible but undeniably present. Listening to this insight of our dead is the only chance we have of being caught up in the great gathering of others.

3
The Sea as History and Prophecy
Hew Locke, John Akomfrah, Fabrice Monteiro

Have you ever heard the Zulu story about how Mabassa and Siphiwe soothed their restless children? Believing that their little ones needed stories to calm their discontent, the husband and wife reasoned that since Mabassa, the wood carver, had to hunt for food, then Siphiwe would hunt for narratives. But looking at the world around her, Siphiwe reasoned that she needed to give her children more than once-upon-a-time. She also had to offer them stories of how the world came to be and how they might survive its meanness. So, to the baboon Mfene, the owl Khova, the hippopotamus Nvuba, and the fish-eagle Inkwazi she went in search of narratives, but none of the animals could be bothered. After some time, she traveled to the edge of the ocean and beseeched the sea turtle Ufudu. "Can you help me?" she said. "My husband and I need stories for our children, stories that will not only entertain but also enlighten." Ufudu instructed Siphiwe to climb on her back, and down the turtle took her to the bottom of the sea to meet the Spirit People who were sitting among lustrous shells and coral. Discovering—to her amazement—that she could breathe under water, Siphiwe asked the King and Queen of the sea-city if they had any stories that they could spare. The King and Queen responded by saying that they did, particularly ones with the properties that Siphiwe desired. But they would require payment in kind. For they had never seen the world above the waters, and in exchange for the stories, Siphiwe would have to bring them something from that world. She promptly bowed to the King and Queen and hurried on Ufudu's back. When she made it home, she told Mabassa of her plan, and traveled once again to the Spirit World with a bundle in her arms. The packet comprised Mabassa's carvings, each one a likeness of Mfene the baboon, Khova the owl, Nvuba the hippopotamus, Inkwazi the fish-eagle, and all the other animals that roamed the world above the currents. Thrilled by these gifts, the King and Queen presented Siphiwe with a shell. "Whenever you have need of stories, press the shell to your ear," they told her. That evening, as her family sat around the fire and as the children began to grow restless again, Siphiwe put the shell to her ear, and furnished them with a tale to inspire and enlighten.

This tale presents the sea as the giver of stories and the embracer of art. In addition, the myth offers lessons about how visual works and narrative can help broker ties between land and ocean. It is also a parable about how the human and the more-than-human can find kinship with one another. Therefore, in the spirit of Siphiwe's gesture, this chapter extends the artworks of Hew Locke, John Akomfrah, and Fabrice Monteiro in exchange for the sea's stories about empire, race, and capitalism.

In the sea's vast waters, we can find linkages and disruptions of global proportions, ones involving enslaved people, refugees, pirates, migrants, and underwater creatures. In addition to being a highway on which a multitude of life-forms travel, the sea is also the domain of grand exploitations perpetrated by powerful nation-states and multinational corporations. Indeed, slavery, colonialism, imperialism, neocolonialism, and neoliberalism have become part of the water's burden. And in the sea's battered visage, we can measure the health of our world. Through the works of these artists and following these aspects of the sea, this chapter argues for models of black radicalism that can hold in awareness the social formations and histories that the waters endure.

For Those in Peril on the Sea

The sea links people. That's what motivated Hew Locke's 2011 exhibition *For Those in Peril on the Sea* (see figure 18). In an effort to address the situation of refugees and the particular dangers that the sea poses to them, the British Guyanese artist built seventy-nine model-sized boats of various sizes and housed the installation at the Perez Art Museum in Miami. The museum describes the installation this way:

> Consisting of dozens of scaled-down replicas of ships suspended from the ceiling, the installation creates the impression of a massive exodus taking place throughout the architectural space above the viewer. It features a broad range of vessel types, from cigarette boats, catamarans, and cruise liners to ragged fishing skiffs and timeworn cargo ships. In light of Miami's history as the site for numerous waves of immigration—particularly from the Caribbean, and specifically by sea—*For Those in Peril on the Sea* will have a particular resonance for the Museum's audiences.[1]

The installation invokes not only the journeys of refugees but of multinational corporations as well. Indeed, in the exhibition are the presumed major and minor protagonists of contemporary globalization. For Locke, the installation represents "[what] people will do and what people will cobble together to get themselves from one place . . . to Miami."[2] Locke uses the boats to redefine Miami as a site of migration, refugeeism, and

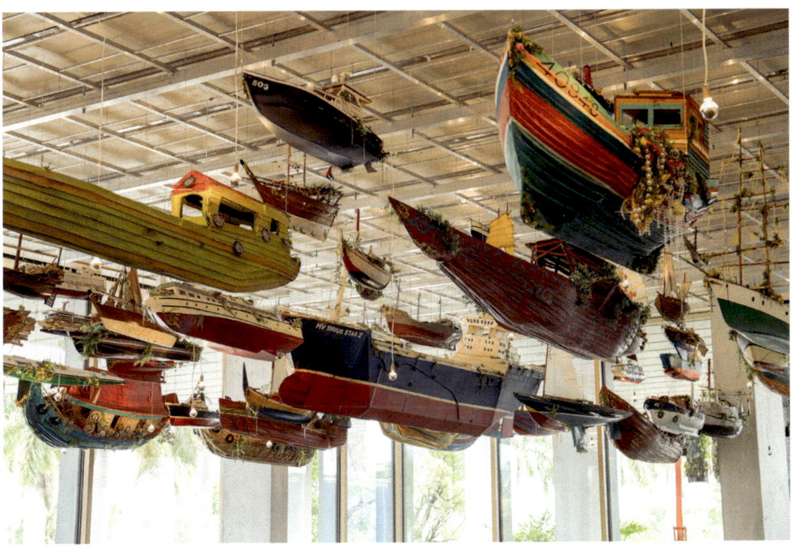

Figure 18. Hew Locke. *For Those in Peril on the Sea*. 2011. Mixed media.

globalization. The installation tells the story of globalization rendered from the perspective of those it sets adrift.

Locke's title is taken from a hymn titled "Eternal Father, Strong to Save," written by the British hymnist William Whiting in 1860. Surviving a raging storm while on a voyage at sea, Whiting wrote the hymn believed to be inspired by the story of the ocean's power found in Psalm 107:

> Some went out on the sea in ships; they were merchants on the
> mighty waters.
> They saw the works of the Lord, his wonderful deeds in the deep.
> For he spoke and stirred up a tempest that lifted high the waves.
> They mounted up to the heavens and went down to the depths;
> in their peril their courage melted away.[3]

The psalm tells a familiar biblical story in which human beings are humbled by the power of God as witnessed through nature. Whiting would evoke that power in the hymn as well:

> ETERNAL FATHER, strong to save,
> whose arm hath bound the restless wave,
> Who bid'st the mighty ocean deep
> Its own appointed limits keep;
> O hear us when we cry to Thee
> For those in peril on the sea.[4]

Whiting's song was popularized by navies in the UK and the United States. Rather than invoke the hymn to consecrate the military, however, Locke would cite it to bless the lives of migrants.

As a matter of fact, *For Those in Peril on the Sea* was partly inspired by the tradition of hanging votive ships from the ceilings of European cathedrals and churches, but Locke brings a more contemporary urgency to the tradition, one that has to do with the precarious existence of migrants and refugees, those groups of people who are left unsung by nation-states. Locke was particularly interested in Miami as a city that has received Caribbean migrants seeking a better life. He says, for instance, that the installation is a "contemporary global take as well as a contemporary Caribbean take . . . with specific aspects relating to Miami."[5] About the ships that he made for the exhibition, Locke says, "They are all a variation on the idea that, wherever we come from, we are all in this thing together: there but for the grace of God go you and I."[6]

The colors of the boats in the exhibition resemble those from the flags of various Caribbean nations. There are the greens, yellows, and reds of the flags of Grenada and Guyana. Then there are the reds, whites, and blues of Puerto Rico, Cuba, Costa Rica, Panama, Haiti, and Belize. There are also the cerulean blue, yellow, white, and black of the Saint Lucian flag. The colors might be understood as symbols of the migrants' roots, the bits and pieces of national cultures that migrants carry with them on their scattered journeys.

About the variety of ships in the installation, Locke says, "There are oil tankers and there are Arab Dhows, and boats based on those refugees get in to cross the Atlantic from Senegal to the Canary Islands, and there are rafts, and there are Japanese boats based loosely on the Tsunami images."[7] In their various sizes, the ships in *For Those in Peril on the Sea* represent the different entities—peoples and corporations—that make their way on the oceans' waves. For the Black British intellectual Stuart Hall, contemporary globalization is characterized by what he calls "the astonishing late twentieth-century, early twenty-first-century movement of dispersed peoples."[8] This dispersion is made up of "the economic migrants and the asylum seekers, the illegal immigrants, the '*sans papiers*,' the ones without proper papers. The ones driven into the camps across the borders by famine, civil war, environmental devastation, or pandemic. A movement of people trying never to be 'there' crossing every boundary in the world."[9] We might say that Locke's installation represents how contemporary globalization upheaves the lives of everyday people.

But globalization, as Hall states, is not only the migrant's story. It is capitalism's story as well. Contemporary globalization (or "neoliberalism," as we currently call it) signifies a clash between the global differences of the subjugated and the global power of financial markets and corporations. It denotes the ways that global markets and corporations have capitalized on nations and peoples in the global south, extracting on massive scales all that they could in the way of labor and natural resources, producing global structural inequalities in which "deregulated financial markets"[10] create "global capital and currency flows large enough to destabilize medium-sized economies."[11] These levels of exploitation would lead to the mass exoduses of displaced people. As the scholar Iain Chambers argues, "If modernity—from voyages of discovery, foreign conquest, global trade and planetary financial flows—is all about mobility and the perpetual movement of goods and capital, it is equally, and inevitably, also about the migration of bodies, lives, cultures and histories. One comes with the other."[12]

In the installation, for instance, you can find a model of the *MV Sirius Star* (see figure 19), the Saudi-owned oil tanker that was highjacked by Somali pirates in 2011 off the coast of Somalia. Locke's *MV Sirius Star* is one of his largest boats. Noting the significance of the hijacking, Locke said, "It was the largest tanker at the time that Somali pirates had gotten hold of. It was carrying crude oil and worth millions."[13]

Although the tanker was owned by the Saudis, it was registered by the Liberian government; hence, the model tanker, like its real-life counterpart, is painted red, white, and blue—the colors of the Liberian flag. Why would a Saudi-owned vessel be painted in the colors of another nation? The answer lies in a peculiar practice called the flag of convenience. The flag

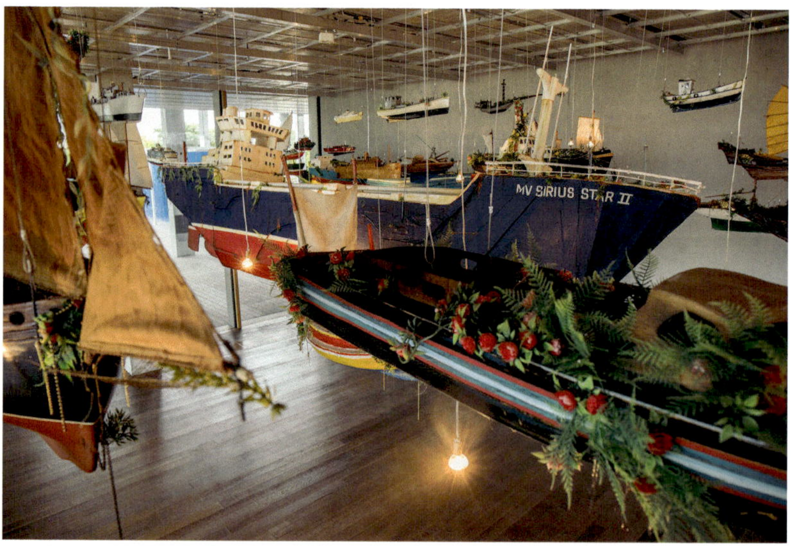

Figure 19. Hew Locke. *MV Sirius Star*. In *For Those in Peril on the Sea*. 2011. Mixed media.

of convenience, or FOC, is an artifact of global deregulation. As the scholar Laleh Khalili argues, "To sail under a flag of a country transforms the ship into a quantum of sovereignty of that country."[14] Typically associated with countries with lax regulations, flags of convenience are used by powerful nations and corporations to evade laws and cut "costs to benefit trade and profits."[15] Flags of convenience originated in US machinations. Khalili writes, for instance, "The establishment of Liberia's registry occurred under the auspices of the former US Secretary of State and ambassador to the United Nations, the patrician Edward Stettinius, who took his extensive transnational connections to making a tidy profit from colonial exploitation of Liberian resources."[16] Flags of convenience would facilitate shadowy business dealings in which wealthy governments and corporations could exploit the resources and vulnerabilities of lesser nations.

By keeping the focus on the act of piracy, attention was taken away from the FOC and what it permitted. During the hijacking, for instance, media characterized the pirates as engaging in a series of "brazen attacks," with the capture of the *Sirius* the most recent outrage at the time. Then–Saudi foreign minister Prince Saud al-Faisal said, "Piracy, like terrorism, is a disease which is against everybody, and everybody must address it together."[17] Hence, the pirates were cast on the side of wrong, while the ships and the Saudi government were framed as the morally upright victims.[18] As the FOCs suggest, though, there was a bigger criminal enterprise taking place, one that exceeded what the Somali pirates could accomplish. That enterprise involved the *MV Sirius Star* and the ways that the FOCs had turned the seas into a foundry of crimes of global proportion. As one former economic adviser put it, "Offshore secrecy encourages and facilitates crime on an industrial scale, and a vast pinstripe infrastructure of lawyers, accountants and bankers profits handsomely from handling illicit transactions."[19] The most powerful countries in the world are participants in this secret network, a network that ensnares the world's most vulnerable peoples.

For Those in Peril on the Sea captures these two aspects of globalization—those parts of it that arise from multinational capital and those elements of it that arise from the dispersion of the desperate, from the "untold tens of thousands of refugees, migrants, and their children . . . consigned to horrific, unnatural, premature deaths by shipwreck and drowning, often following protracted ordeals of abandonment at sea,"[20] in the words of cultural studies scholar Nicholas de Genova. The installation then asks its viewers to see what injustices and tragedies happen way out in the water.

For the art historian Claire Bishop, installation art attempts to "activate" viewers by encouraging them to engage with the world. Concurrently, she argues, installation art also works to "decenter" the viewer. By this she means that installation art "denies the viewer any one ideal place from which to survey the work."[21] This de-centering in Locke's work is not due to abstraction but because of the baroque and processual nature of the work. Discussing the kinetic nature of his work, Locke says, "Migration, movement of people from one place to another and what they bring with them, will continue to be a strong theme in my work, because it's everything."[22] Taking his inspiration from the votive boats hanging in European cathedrals, Locke positions the viewer from the vantage point of the parishioner whose prayers are lifted up to the people who symbolically inhabit the boats hanging above. In this way, the viewer becomes the hymnist and supplicant singing and praying for the migrants caught in the sea's convulsions, in the global market's exploitation, and in the nation-state's failures.

Like the other artworks discussed in this chapter, the sea in Locke's installation becomes the symbol of those histories and experiences that need to be raised from the deep. *For Those in Peril on the Sea* invokes the lives that were lost unnaturally in the water's torrents. In doing so, the installation calls for a black radical tradition that identifies the refugee crisis as part of its critical mission.

Akomfrah's *Vertigo Sea*

He was interested in several narratives and identities coming together. That's why John Akomfrah made the 2015 video installation *Vertigo Sea*. Like Locke's installation, *Vertigo Sea* calls for a kind of immersion as well. Akomfrah's installation is placed on three adjoining screens and uses fragments of literature, archival materials, underwater footage, and historical reenactments to address the ocean as a site of natural beauty and historic terrors. It immerses viewers in such topics as transatlantic slavery, whaling, migration, refugeeism, Islamophobia, colonialism, political imprisonment, and the lives of sea creatures.

According to Akomfrah, the French filmmaker Chris Marker's interest in Alfred Hitchcock's 1958 classic *Vertigo* partly inspired the installation. As Akomfrah says, "The title *Vertigo Sea* is very much a crib from the Hitchcock film—but as channeled by Chris Marker. Marker was the one who introduced most of my generation to that classic in the early 1980s. His diagnosis of it as a portrait of derangement, of masculine excess, and of a certain kind of mania for control and possession, is what I allude to with this piece."[23] Indeed, *Vertigo Sea* alludes to that mania via the history of the sea as the playground of Western might.

With its scenes of people in colonial garb settling on new territory, of enslaved Africans thrown overboard, and of radio accounts of the current plight of refugees, *Vertigo Sea* dramatizes how the sea is the history of mastery and manhood as well as the subjugation and unmaking of peoples around the globe. A voice-over recites a line from Herman Melville's *Moby-Dick* as the installation depicts scenes of a uniformed man standing on a rocky precipice overlooking icebergs. The man's pose recalls Caspar David Friedrich's *The Wanderer above the Sea of Fog* and invokes the fabled attributes of Western man: "What I've dared," the voice pronounces, "I've willed; and what I've willed, I'll do."

In the history of the West, mastery and will have been matters not only pertaining to land but to the sea as well. In 1608, the Dutch philosopher, jurist, and political theorist Hugo Grotius, for instance, wrote the influential book *Mare Liberum (On the Freedom of the Seas)* with the sea's global reorganization in mind. The book rebutted the Portuguese claim that they alone controlled trade in East and Southeast Asia and India. For the artist and theorist Allen Sekula, the book promoted the idea that the sea "[exceeds] and even [resists] terrestrial boundaries and national proprietary claims."[24] In fact, Grotius wrote the book in response to Portugal's monopoly on the sea as a trade site.[25] The sea, he said, belonged to no one and was therefore open to everyone. As he wrote,

> Can the vast, the boundless sea be the appendage of one nation alone, and it not the greatest? Can any one nation have the right to prevent other nations which so desire, from selling to one another, from bartering with one another, actually from communicating with one another? Can any nation give away what it never owned,

> or discover what already belonged to some one else? Does a manifest injustice of long standing create a specific right?[26]

For Grotius, equal access to the sea represented commercial fairness for all Western nations. He asserted, "The subjects of the United Netherlands . . . have the right to sail to the East Indies, as they are now doing, and to engage in trade with the people there. . . . Every nation is free to travel to every other nation, and to trade with it."[27] For Grotius, establishing the sea as a free and open space was a way of ensuring that European trade and markets would flow freely. As he said, "For do not the ocean, navigable in every direction with which God has encompassed all the earth, and the regular and the occasional winds which blow now from one quarter and now from another, offer sufficient proof that Nature has given to all peoples a right of access to all other peoples."[28]

The Dutch were active members of the slave trade in the Atlantic and Indian Oceans during the seventeenth and eighteenth centuries.[29] Indeed, according to the historian Markus Vink, the Dutch drew parts of East Africa, the Mascarene Islands of Mauritius and Réunion, South Asia, and South East Asia into its web of enslavement. When the Dutch conquered Northern Brazil in 1630, their trade in the Atlantic Ocean would begin in earnest. Grotius's dream of free and open waters would culminate in turning the seas into a network of pathways for trading both goods and bodies.

Historian Stephanie Smallwood contextualizes the struggle over who had a right to the sea as a contest that, after the publication of Grotius's book, had the slave trade as its stake and multiple European nations as its players. She writes, "Over the course of the seventeenth century, what had been an exclusively Portuguese arena became a site of close competition among European colonizing nations, as French, Dutch, and English incursions challenged the Portuguese claim to a monopoly on European trade in Africa."[30] In this outrageous contest, there is little wonder why a human being aboard a slave ship would be measured alongside rice, tar, and turpentine.

As the scholar Christina Sharpe argues, slavery continues its signs and symbols "from the forced movements of the enslaved to the forced movements of the migrant and the refugee, to the regulation of Black people in North American streets and neighborhoods, to those ongoing crossings

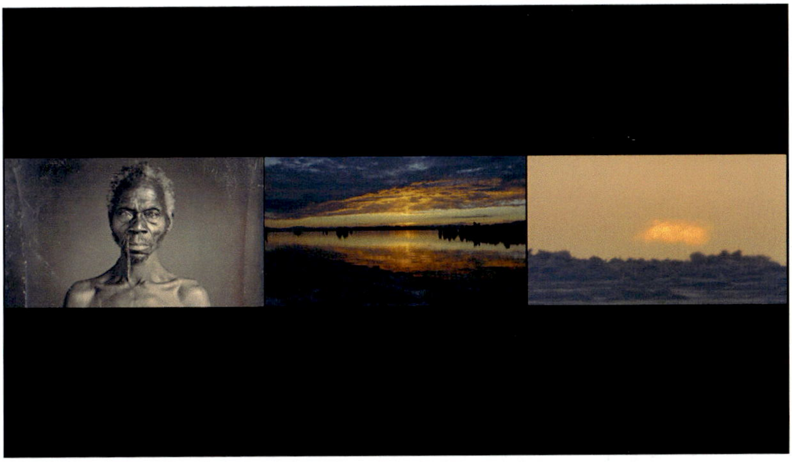

Figure 20. John Akomfrah. *Vertigo Sea. Renty and Landscapes.* 2015. Three channel HD color video installation, 7.1 sound, 48 minutes 30 seconds. Lisson Gallery. Los Angeles. Reprinted with permission.

of and drownings in the Mediterranean Sea, to the brutal colonial reimaginings of the slave ship and the ark."[31] In *Vertigo Sea*, we see an image of an enslaved man named Renty (see figure 20) on one screen. We don't know much about him, only that his daguerreotype was found in the attic of the Peabody Museum in Cambridge, Massachusetts, in 1976 along with fourteen other photos of enslaved Black persons. Several of the photographs had labels attached to them, identifying the names of the people photographed, along with their assumed ethnic group, and the people who owned them. Renty was believed to have come from the Congo. The pictures date back to 1850 and were made for the Swiss naturalist and later Harvard professor Louis Agassiz. As the historian Molly Rogers argues, the photographs would represent an early and curious meeting of photography and ethnology.[32] This encounter would represent another peculiar partnership—one between slavery and natural history, a partnership that would classify Black people on the lower rungs of humanity and affix them to the degraded labors of slavery. The photos would, in sum, be used to attempt to prove that Black people were not only physically different from whites but morally distinct as well.

Renty's photograph was supposed to prove that he was an inferior being. Emaciated, he faces out, staring at the viewer. The middle screen shows a sunrise on the water. The third screen depicts a sunset. Together, they present a triptych of degradations that stretch from sunrise to sunset. By putting Renty and the water next to one another, *Vertigo Sea* implicates the ocean in Renty's predicament, and his body bears witness to the calculated violence that extends from the sea to the plantation.

One of the writers who played a "supporting role" in *Vertigo Sea* is the Saint Lucian poet and playwright Derek Walcott. In particular, Walcott's poem "The Sea Is History" inspired Akomfrah to reckon with the sea's role in the annals of human atrocities. In the poem, an unknown querent asks an African ancestor a series of questions. The first one is,

> Where are your monuments, your battles, martyrs?
> Where is your tribal memory?

The ancestor responds,

> Sirs, in that gray vault. The sea. The sea
> has locked them up. The sea is history.[33]

Later on, the same querent ventures another question:

> Where is your renaissance?

The ancestor responds generously,

> Sir, it is locked in them sea-sands
> out there past the reef's moiling shelf,
> where the men-o'-war floated down;
> strop on these goggles, I'll guide you there myself.[34]

With the ancestor's offer to guide the querent through the water's depths, the ancestor becomes like the turtle in Siphiwe's story. Taking the querent down below the surface, the ancestor reveals that the only way to appreciate this history is to take seriously the worlds beneath the waters. And as the ancestor helps the querent dive into the water's mysteries, so *Vertigo Sea* helps the viewer descend as well.

In *Fish Story*, Sekula wrote that people who live near harbors have certain quaint assumptions about the global economy. Because of their proximity to the sea, they believe that the global economy can be "seen and heard and smelled."[35] For those people close to the sea, "The wealth of nations [slides] in by the channel." This is the history of the sea from the vantage of those who were born of the harbor rather than the ones who were brought to it. In Walcott's poem, those who were brought against their will point to the smells and sounds that connoted the global economy that was the slave trade. As the ancestor states,

> First there was the heaving oil,
> heavy as chaos;
> then, like a light at the end of the tunnel,
> the lantern of a caravel,
> and that was Genesis.
> Then there were the packed cries,
> the shit, the moaning: Exodus.[36]

The caravel is the Portuguese sailing ship that allowed the Portuguese to explore the west coast of Africa, a nautical innovation that would facilitate Portugal's involvement in the slave trade.

This innovation would give birth to the early global economy, one that relied heavily on maritime invention for the exploration of new trading possibilities and the opening of new markets. That new economy also gave birth to innovations in bodily cruelty and human degradation. Distinguishing the fabled ship of the Bible from its modern counterpart, Sekula wrote, "The Ark is no longer a bestiary but an encyclopedia of trade and industry."[37] For the slave ship, its encyclopedic entries were made up of people, packed with guns, gunpowder, knives, textiles, and gold. As Smallwood argues, "[Slaves] became, for the purpose of transatlantic shipment, mere physical units that could be arranged and molded at will—whether folded spoonlike in rows or flattened side by side in a plane."[38]

In addition to being the places where bodies and merchandise could be transported as part of the same peculiar inventory, the sea has also been the domain of curious encounters between humans and the creatures of the sea. *Vertigo Sea* attempts to make a history of those encounters. In the film the wretched of both the earth and the sea contend with how nations and capitalism have caused both to fight for their lives. Akomfrah heard a story of a young Nigerian man who crossed the Mediterranean out of desperation. Relating the refugee's tale, he said, "Here's a figure who walked from the rainforest of West Africa onto a boat that then shipwrecked and now he is about to die. And in that moment he becomes a new person."[39]

Part of what makes the young man into a "new person" is that he is not alone in his trials. Akomfrah states, "[Yes], it's about the Nigerian, but it is also about the millions of tuna in the cage that he's hanging onto for dear life. They are also literally clinging on for dear life. How do we get that commonwealth of beings on the same stage at the same time?"[40] While the tuna were being turned into commodities whose value was being determined by the fishing industry, the young Nigerian was being turned into a refugee whose value would be decided by where he landed and where he worked.

In the installation, one panel shows scenes of those same Africans who were thrown overboard washing up on the shore. Another screen uses archival footage to depict whales gutted by hunters. In doing so, Akomfrah takes the story of the young Nigerian and the tuna and recasts it in the histories of colonial slavery and whaling, making the people and the whales the victims of a system bent on their destruction (see figure 21). By placing

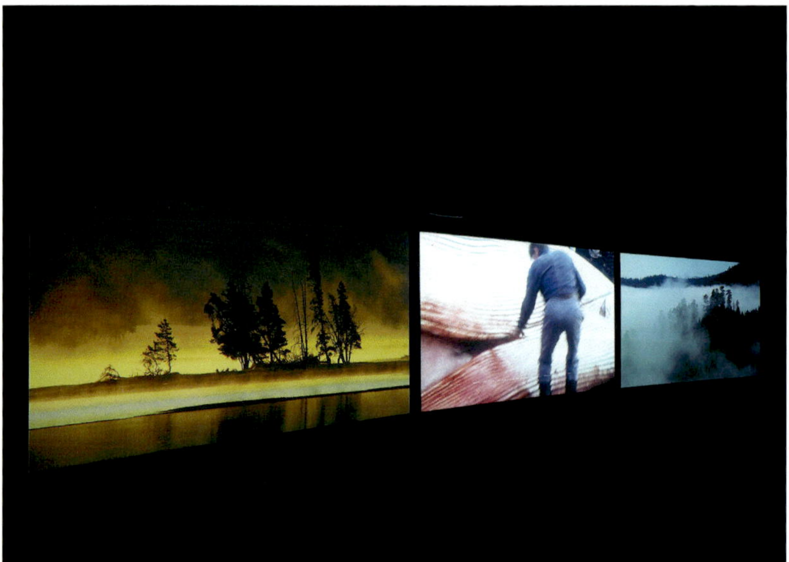

Figure 21. John Akomfrah. *Vertigo Sea. Whaling and Landscapes.* 2015. Three channel HD color video installation, 7.1 sound, 48 minutes 30 seconds. Lisson Gallery. Los Angeles. Reprinted with permission.

them together, *Vertigo Sea* puts this "commonwealth" on the same historical stage, one in which the atrocities suffered by humans are part of the system that devastates animal life.

Akomfrah must have really heard the ancestor in Walcott's poem talk of the moment when history truly began, that time when "each rock broke into its own nation," when the "secretarial heron" and the "synod of flies" came and the bullfrog "[bellowed] for a vote."[41] The ancestor shows the querent the communities that take shape among the nonhuman. *Vertigo Sea* shows the viewer the societies that the stingrays, whales, and polar bears have produced, suggesting the intelligence that they have marshaled to do so. Rather than set the relations between humans and nonhumans as one of antagonists or competitors, the installation frames the colonized and the dispossessed as descriptions that capture certain humans and nonhumans alike. As Akomfrah noted, "[The] overriding concern for *Vertigo Sea* . . . [was] to construct a theatrical space with a stage made up of different species, some human and not human. To avoid a moral hierarchy in which whales are less important than people."[42] In *Vertigo Sea*, Akomfrah attempts to alter the collective consciousness so that the sea becomes the history of race and colonization with respect to both persons and animals.

In *Black Marxism*, Cedric Robinson wrote that the Black radical tradition was a way of continually developing "a collective consciousness informed by the historical struggles for liberation and motivated by the shared sense of obligation to preserve the collective being, the ontological totality."[43] Read as an intervention into Black radical traditions, *Vertigo Sea* tries to expand our collective consciousness by asking, "What is our obligation to preserve our human and nonhuman collective being from the social forces that threaten all our well-being?" This reformulated Black radical tradition would assume the protection and rescue of different species as part of its revolutionary charge.[44]

The kind of reorientation that *Vertigo Sea* calls for requires that we confront the biases that have constituted much of our radical traditions. The environmental and African Studies scholar Cajetan Iheka argues that anticolonial struggles typically privileged the human as the object of emancipation. As he says, "The quest for decolonization and national liberation trumped other considerations including questions of patriarchy and women's rights. The environment did not merit inclusion at all."[45]

Iheka posits the stories, beliefs, and sacred practices of Indigenous cultures in Africa as models of ethical interactions between humans and nonhumans. Along with *Vertigo Sea*, these Indigenous engagements might be the sources of inspiration for Black radical traditions that throw down their historic privileging of human realities over nonhuman ones. This would mean evolving traditions that—to use Iheka's words—"yoke together obligations to both constituencies and position these responsibilities at the heart of what it means to be human."[46]

Evolving such traditions would mean creating social contracts different from the one handed to us through the dominant paradigms of Western philosophy and politics. In a discussion of Rousseau's social contract, the Black environmental and critical ethnic studies scholar David Pellow says, "Through what Rousseau called the social contract, 'subpersons' and 'savages' were excluded from the polity since they were equated with nature. Thus, nature and the spaces certain people (or 'subpersons') occupied were devalued, or perhaps selectively valued insofar as they provided a strategic benefit to the modernity project."[47] This devaluing would have devastating repercussions for humans and nonhumans. As Pellow argues, "[The] meaning of space and race codeveloped to produce racism and environmental harm as one integrated process as European expansion took hold during the sixteenth century. In other words, the ideological, cultural, psychological, and physical harm visited on people of color was supported and made possible by a system that did the same to nature." While the histories of racism and environmental harm were integrated, we still have yet to produce political and intellectual models that integrate those histories. Yet as *Vertigo Sea* juxtaposes the hunting of whales and polar bears alongside the histories of enslavement and refugeeism, it calls for a Black radical tradition that can hold all of these histories together, one that can be like that ancestor who can talk about a commonwealth made up not only of people but also of creeping, flying, and swimming things.

Fabrice Monteiro's *The Prophecy*

In *The Prophecy*, a series by the Beninese photographer Fabrice Monteiro, the goddess Gaia sends her djinns to issue a set of warnings to humankind. The wide-bosomed mother of the earth has grown weary of trying to maintain the planet's natural cycles against the ravages of environmental violence. In an attempt to put them back on course, she sends her djinns with revelations to the world above. *The Prophecy* depicts the story of the djinn's assignment. In this peril, as with the others, the sea plays a central role. Indeed, if Locke's installation turned its viewers into underwater witnesses, and if Akomfrah's piece transformed its onlookers into ancestral narrators, then *The Prophecy* casts its viewers as second-sighted observers.

Monteiro grew up in Benin and is based in Dakar, Senegal. The series came to him as a way to address environmental problems in Africa. Eschewing a realist depiction of environmental catastrophes, he chose a medium that instead would resonate with everyday Senegalese people. His decision to go with an indigenous framework for the series was based on his observations of NGOs trying to intervene in environmental struggles. About those NGOs he said, "They come with ideas that are already made, and the people there don't get it, because it doesn't talk to them. But using animism, the whole of West Africa believes in the spirits, and the idea was to use the spirits to deliver a message."[48]

Monteiro joined forces with the Senegalese fashion designer Doulsy to create the djinns that make up the series. About the collaboration, Monteiro said, "I came up with the idea, and I said, 'Ok, we're going to talk to that subject, and we're going to do a costume that is going to look like a tree limb.'" Monteiro's time in the fashion industry assisted him with *The Prophecy*. As he said, "I decided to create photography that would look more like me. Which is, on one side, this fashion background that I had—and then my African childhood, and my vision of this continent, and so the fact that I'm mixed. I have this African culture from my [Beninese] father, and European culture from my [Belgian] mother."[49] Monteiro would also use the series to unite politics and aesthetics, or as he put it, to use the series as a "bridge between fashion photography and doing photography that's useful."[50] And as with the other artists, the sea looms large in *The Prophecy*.

In one of the photographs, a djinn has made herself visible and emerges from the water, wearing a black gown covered in oil, her beauty marred by the oil that coats her (see figure 22). The stomacher of her gown is made up of white bird feathers, but the other parts of her gown have been littered with the feathers of birds that have become the casualties of an oil spill, evidenced by the capsized boat in the distance. The giant djinn carries a dead bird in her left hand, its feathers coated with oil. In a state of shock,

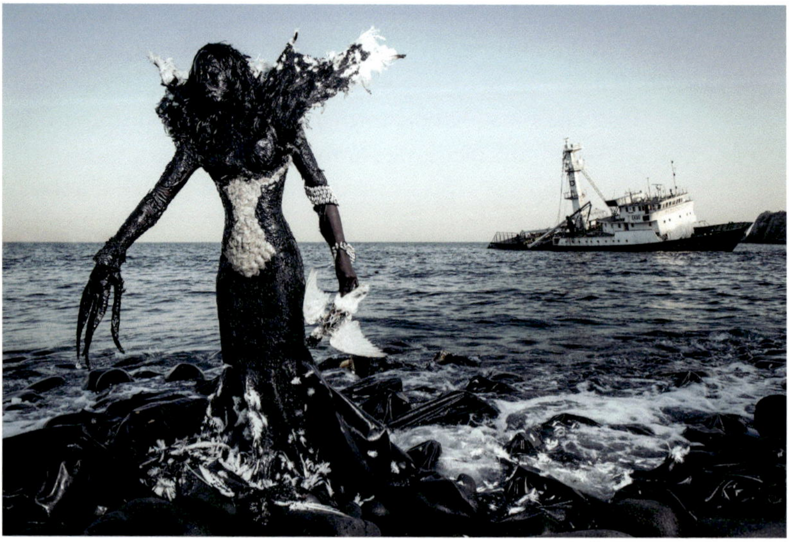

Figure 22. Fabrice Monteiro. *The Prophecy. Oil Spill Djinn*. 2013. Fabrice Monteiro/Institute. Reprinted with permission.

she slouches through a domain that she has known for millennia. The oil spill has caused an unprecedented outrage, disturbing worldly and spiritual orders, putting everything in jeopardy.

The scholar John S. Mbiti wrote in his classic *Introduction to African Religion*, "[According] to African views, the universe is composed of visible and invisible parts. It is commonly believed that, besides God and human beings there are other beings who populate the universe. These are the spirits."[51] Monteiro's djinns are composites of Arab and Islamic mythology and Indigenous folklore, but he replaces a patriarchal God with a maternal one; in doing so, he suggests that environmental pollution does not represent the castration of our Father but the violation of our Mother. In fact, Gaia's djinns represent those spirits that are "associated with the things and forces of the earth. These are the forces and things closest to human life."[52] As part of the forces and things closest to human life, they bring a particular message to humans about how our most intimate relationship with the earth has been devastated.

The Prophecy forces the viewer to see that devastation. In addition, Monteiro compels the viewer to confront how nonhuman life and spiritual existence are jeopardized too. By doing so, the series upsets the privilege given to humans as the center of the social world. Discussing the ways that humans have occupied this center in philosophical and social thought, Iheka argues, "The anthropocentric position, under which ecological violence has become normalized, places humans at the center of the universe and sanctions those activities meant to 'prosper' the human, even when they are detrimental to other beings."[53] To challenge the ways that ecological violence has become normal, *The Prophecy* knocks the human from his vaunted place and asks us to see the catastrophe through the ancient eyes of the djinns.

The djinn who is covered in oil has a message about our dependence on it as a fuel. To begin with, oil has brought particular dangers to African cities. The geographer Michael Watts argues that African cities "stand as hubs within a vast regional (and ultimately global) network of oil 'hardware.'"[54] Those cities are homes to oil refineries, petrochemical mills, gas plants, and the legion of workers that work in them. Discussing what this "global oil and gas infrastructure" has wrought for the planet and the seas, Watts says, "Close to one million producing oil wells puncture the surface of the earth (77,000 were drilled in 2008, 4,000 offshore); 3,300 are subsea, puncturing the earth's crust on the continental shelf in some cases thousands of metres below the ocean's surface."[55] Watts observes that astonishingly, "[More] than 2 million kilometres of pipelines blanket the globe in a massive trunk network."[56] For the djinn and the dead bird that she holds, this "massive trunk network" is a corruption of dire consequence.

Talking about the persuasive power of a photograph, the noted French film critic André Bazin said, "In spite of any objections our critical spirit may offer, we are forced to accept as real the existence of the object reproduced, actually, re-presented, set before us . . . in time and space."[57] Monteiro's photographs of defiled orishas ask the viewer to accept the reality of environmental devastation and its deeply spiritual consequences. He sets before us the fact of environmental catastrophes and spiritual desecration, asking the viewer to bear witness to and cry out against those violations.

In her classic text *On Photography*, Susan Sontag argued, "Photographs actively promote nostalgia. . . . All photographs are memento mori. To take a photograph is to participate in another person's (or thing's) mortality, vulnerability, mutability."[58] *The Prophecy* asks us to participate in the vulnerability of the environment, but it does not do so by recourse to nostalgia. There is no elegy of the already dead, but there is a panic over a world that is at death's door, a panic that the series hopes to be the basis of some leap into action.

In another photo (see figure 23), a Minerva-like djinn stands on the shores of a beach. She's tall and soldierly, holding a shield made of a tortoise shell. Her face and her plumed headdress are blackened by what appears to be oil. Her bodice is a breastplate made of seashells, and her left arm is covered by the silver manica worn by gladiators. Her skirt is made up of a green net embellished with the sea's garbage—bits of plastic, dead sea animals, clothes, shells, a claw, and so on. She drags yet another net behind her with more of the sea's litter entangled in it. Intent on her purpose, she seems to have come from some expedition the aim of which is to clean the sea's contaminated waters.

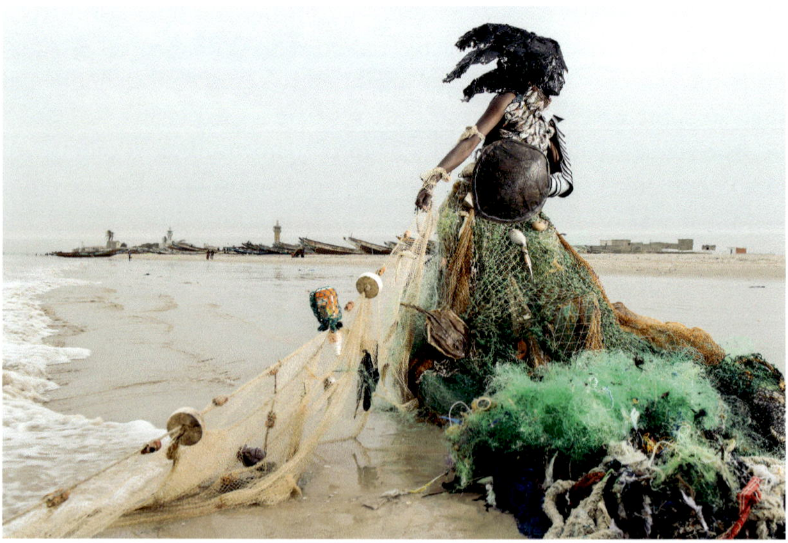

Figure 23. Fabrice Monteiro. *The Prophecy. Ghost Nets Djinn*. 2013. Fabrice Monteiro/Institute. Reprinted with permission.

Her costume and her errand refer to the pollution caused by the fishing industry. According to the environmental organization Greenpeace, over "640,000 tonnes of nets, lines, pots, and traps used in commercial fishing are dumped into the sea every year."[59] This "ghost gear" accounts for 10 percent of marine litter, threatens marine life, divers, and fishermen, and it clogs harbors. Between 2002 and 2010, 872 nets containing 32,000 marine animals were recovered from the state of Washington alone.[60] Unregulated industry and overcrowded fishing account for ghost gear as a worldwide and world-devastating phenomenon. According to a 2019 Greenpeace Report, "Poor regulation and slow political progress in creating ocean sanctuaries that are off-limits to industrial fishing allow this problem to exist and persist."[61] The report goes on to say, "Even worse, in international waters there is currently no comprehensive legal framework in place to protect marine life and ocean health."[62] We could read the tortoise shield that the djinn carries and the ghost gear that she wears and drags as symbols of all that the waters must negotiate because of deregulation.

Monteiro's mix of the fantastic and the tragic has roots not only in Indigenous African cultures and Islamic mythology but in surrealism as well. Indeed, his compositions deploy some of the surrealist techniques of fashion photography. By way of history, surrealism influenced fashion photography as photographers upended photographic conventions by taking "recognizable objects" out of their "normal context and recombining [them] in fantastic ways."[63] The costumes that Doulsy created are literally made from recognizable objects taken out of their normal contexts and superimposed onto clothing. Affixed with shells, fishing gear, crab claws, tortoise shells, bottles, feathers, oil, and so on, the costumes direct the viewer's eye to the devastated background from which the costumes come. As such, the djinns' costumes make the clothes a starting point from which to observe the environmental crisis.

The photographic aesthetics in Monteiro's series mesh with the surrealist aspects of Black radical traditions. The historian Robin D. G. Kelley asserts that the "basic principles of surrealism" involved "a living, mutable, creative vision of the world where love, play, human dignity, an end to poverty and want, and imagination are the pillars of freedom."[64] Suzanne Césaire, a leading proponent of surrealism, identified the movement in the 1940s with a critique of Western dominance. She argued, "In art as in life, the surrealist cause is the cause itself of freedom."[65] For Kelley, Black thinkers such as Césaire, her husband Aimé Césaire, and writers and musicians such as Wilfredo Lam, Richard Wright, Frank London Brown, Jayne Cortez, Ted Joans, and Will Alexander "shaped the development of surrealism as a self-conscious political movement."[66]

As *The Prophecy* employs surrealism to address environmental catastrophes, the series invokes Black radical engagements with the destruction of the planet. One exponent of surrealism—the Senegalese painter, poet, and architect Cheikh Tidiane Sylla argued in 1989, for instance, "Surrealism and black African art show that History's last step—the step *beyond* History—coincides with a return to *first principles*, which is also a return to primordial glory, involving nothing less than the systematic and *definitive liberation* of the whole of human society and of Nature itself."[67] We might say that the series "returns to first principles" in its use of the djinns and as it calls for both human and environmental dignity. As an imaginative exercise, *The Prophecy* holds up a vision of freedom in which humans, nonhumans, and the environment must be emancipated from ecological harm. In fact, if we place *The Prophecy* alongside the quote from Sylla and within the history of Black radical traditions, a sustainable environment becomes one of the goals of freedom struggles.

The Prophecy's photographs also point to the vulnerabilities that endanger humans and nonhumans because of contemporary capitalism. The waters are polluted, and the earth is boiling largely because of the actions of corporations. According to a 2017 report from the Carbon Majors Database, "Over half of global industrial emissions since human-induced climate change was officially recognized can be traced to just 25 corporate and state producing entities."[68] As of 1988, the key privately owned companies responsible for those emissions have been ExxonMobil, Shell, BP, Chevron, Peabody, Total, and BHP Billiton. The major state-owned companies are those owned by Saudi Arabia, India, China, Russia, Mexico, and Iran. By organizing their revenue through the extraction of fossil fuels, these companies produce the conditions for jeopardizing all forms of life on earth. Issuing a dire warning, the report asserts, "If the trend in fossil fuel extraction continues over the next 28 years as it has over the previous 28, then global average temperatures would be on course to rise around 4 degrees Celsius above preindustrial levels by the end of the century. This would entail substantial species extinction, large risks of regional and global food scarcity, and could cross multiple tipping points in the Earth's climate system, leading to even more severe consequences."[69] With its scenes of seas and deities damaged by oil and garbage, *The Prophecy* also sounds an alarm about the human and nonhuman costs of corporate extraction.

The French intellectual and activist Françoise Vergès locates environmental devastation within the conjoined legacies of capitalism and colonialism. Addressing colonialism in the Americas and the Caribbean, she writes, "In the reconfiguration of the world that followed the colonization of the Americas and the Caribbean, nature was transformed into a cheap resource, as endlessly renewable as the bonded workforce."[70] Tackling colonialism in Africa, Walter Rodney argued, "One can see in Africa and in Southern Africa in particular the rise of a capitalist super-structure manned by individuals capable of consciously planning the exploitation of resources right into the next century, and aiming at racist domination of black people of Africa until the end of time."[71] The environmental devastation unleashed on contemporary Africa because of privately owned and state-owned corporations continues the legacy of exploitation that Vergès and Rodney highlight. The djinns in *The Prophecy* remind us that—as Vergès puts it—"destruction in the colonial era becomes visible in the postcolonial era."[72] Thus, they reveal the long arc of environmental ruin.

Covering these themes and more, Siphiwe prepared her children for bed and related to them these stories of the great encounters between the human and the nonhuman, between the ephemeral and the eternal, between capital and nature, between corporations and people, and between colonization and freedom. She told them something she learned in her underwater sojourn, that one of the mysteries of the sea is that water is both the balance and the breath of life, and all that upsets the balance and defiles the breath must be fought. There are people fighting for the water's life, she said. One day you too can count yourselves among them. But let us retire, for now, so we can meet all that the next day will bring.

4
Mutations of Militarism and War

Wangechi Mutu

Much of Wangechi Mutu's work is spotted with blood. That's one of the first things that you notice. The other aspects that catch your attention have to do with all the parts that make up the figures in her collages. (See figure 24.) There's the plant-woman-thing, whose high-heeled legs are crowned by a bulb-shaped torso made up of two conjoined women. A bird's beak juts from one of the women's shoulders; two legs playfully kick from atop the swollen trunk. Even more strangely, her back has grown green roots, the ends of which are motorcycle wheels. It's an odd mix of animal, plant, human, and auto parts to be sure, but there's nothing inelegant or Frankenstein-like about it. In fact, the parts seem to communicate with one another, almost like they discovered some way to be together.

This is Kenyan American and Kikuyu artist Wangechi Mutu's 2008 piece *This You Call Civilization*, and it is emblematic of much of her work. Because of its intricacy, her art beggars description. When looking at her pieces, it's not unusual to find yourself asking, "Is it a human, an animal, a plant? How is it all these things at once? What misfortunes have invented these hybrids?" Whatever the answers, you know that—as strangely beautiful as they are—some violence accounts for the odd amalgam of things.

Much of the criticism on Mutu's artwork addresses the histories of colonialism and how those histories have shaped Black women's lives. Extending these examinations, I analyze the possible conditions of violence suggested in her collages, paying particular attention to the ferocity

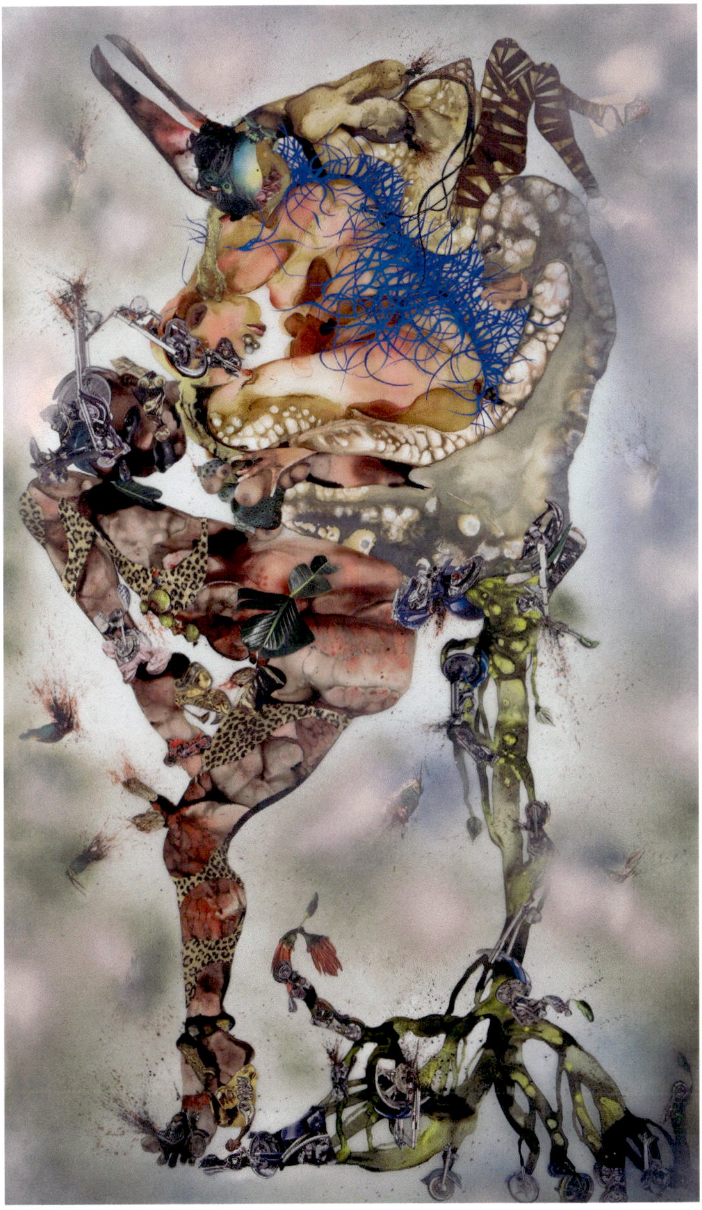

Figure 24. Wangechi Mutu. *This You Call Civilization*. 2008. Mixed media, ink, contact paper on Mylar. 98 x 52 in.

of war—the way it rips communities, bodies, territories, and environments apart and how new associations come out of those conditions. Hence, I put her work in dialogue with Black feminists who have pondered the devastations of militarism and war in not only colonial contexts but anti-colonial and postcolonial ones as well. In doing so, we can discern how Mutu's work joins forces with contemporary feminist writings about how the violence of patriarchy and militarism feed off one another, causing destruction to a variety of worlds.

Mutu and the Memory of British Colonialism

Discussing the region of Kikuyu territory from which her family comes, Mutu says, "The people that I hale [*sic*] from are crop cultivators and landowners. We're farmer people. My family is from Nyeri, the farthest north town of the Gikuyu people."[1] Continuing, she describes the area's topography: "Nyeri is very green land. It is rainy and cool with red, volcanic soil. Mostly highland, it rolls and dives for twenty kilometers up to the base of Mt. Kenya. The town is flanked on both sides by national parks with thick woods, bamboo forests, savannah and waterfalls."[2] Indeed, the diversity of the flora is almost matched by the variety of the region's fauna. As she says, "Black rhinos, leopards and lions saunter right up to your car because of successful controls on poaching in recent years. The elephants are more wary, however, aware of the slaughter of past generations in their strong, collective memory."[3] The abundance of plant and animal life has generated a strong farming culture. According to Mutu, "Cattle and tea and subsistence farms quilt the area. It is a naturally life-giving place; maize, beans, potatoes and vegetables grow easily there. Healthy harvests and abundant water ward off the famines that inflict other parts of the country."[4] This natural wealth made the region a target for colonization.

"The British invaded and occupied this part of Kenya from the late nineteenth century, and thousands of families were forced off of their land,"[5] Mutu observes. Having its appetite whet by the prospect of natural resources, the British empire deployed a variety of colonial maneuvers to satisfy its hunger. Mutu writes, for instance, "In the 1950s, the British forced most of the Gikuyu people out of their homes and interned them in labor camps, barbed-wire villages and prisons. The British conducted 'screenings' in order to determine the extent of the people's sympathies with resistance fighters, which amounted to torture in the form of castration, sodomy and amputations."[6] British colonial forces spared no type of violence—ethnic cleansing, internment, imprisonment, physical and sexual violence—to subdue Mutu's people.

The seeds for this violence were codified years before the British removal of the Kikuyu from their territory. In 1924, for instance, the empire convened the East Africa Commission to visit their African "dependencies"—what is now Northern Zimbabwe, Malawi, Tanzania, Uganda, and Kenya. The commission's job was ostensibly to accelerate the economic and social development of these regions and their peoples, but development really meant increasing British colonial authority and disseminating racist discourses about the Kikuyu. In their 1925 report, the commission stated, "The main problem of East Africa, apart from the further development of transport and communication, which is everywhere inadequate, is the task of furthering the civilisation and productive capacity of the native African inhabitants."[7] For the Commission, East Africans would need to be turned into communities that would submit to the rigors of colonial labor and the biases of colonial ideologies. This ideology constructed Africans as inferior in terms of their capacities for labor, writing, and art. Proposing the benefits of colonialism, the report argued, "The impact of western civilization upon a people who, by themselves, have never evolved a written language, and whose methods of production, whose skill in the arts, and whose social customs are for the most part still primitive, has already been tremendous."[8] Colonialism would, therefore, promise to enhance the colonized economically, socially, intellectually, and spiritually.

According to British colonizers, colonialism would benefit British economic power especially. Referring to the text that became the handbook for British colonial governments, the report asserted, "As Sir Frederick Lugard has pointed out in his well-known book entitled 'The Dual Mandate in British Tropical Africa,' we are not only trustees for the development and advance in civilisation of the African, but we are also trustees for the world of very rich territories. This means that we have a duty to humanity to develop the vast economic resources of a great continent."[9] The British mandate was, thus, an ideology of global proportions, one that claimed administrative and economic authority over much of the planet.

A rapacious identification with Indigenous lands was central to this presumably global duty. As the report said, "[The] economic resources of

East Africa are almost entirely agricultural, and it is therefore to the better use of the soil of Africa that we must look for the means whereby any form of progress can be obtained."[10] It was not enough for British colonial officials to claim other people's territories. Every white British person was supposed to see themselves as trustees of colonialism: "[The] trusteeship lies really upon the shoulders of every man and woman of European race in Africa. It is in very truth a white man's burden, and all Europeans in Africa must share in the work."[11] To complete itself, colonialism had to reconcile white people's minds and hearts with the injustices and cruelties of the system.

In response to colonial invasion, a group of Kikuyu rebels that British settlers dubbed the "Mau Mau" entered the world's stage when they started a movement to seize back the land and freedoms that the British had taken.[12] But the "Mau Mau" entered the limelight amid vilification and misrepresentation. In fact, the word "Mau Mau" exists in no African language, and it was a way of depoliticizing a political struggle against colonialism. If people around the world said "Mau Mau," then they would never learn to say The Kenyan African Union or the Kenya Land and Freedom Army.[13] They would never learn the histories of these groups whose political objective was to win rights and reclaim stolen territory for the peoples of Kenya.

But "Mau Mau" proved to be an effective propaganda device. As the historian Caroline Elkins notes, "From the start of the war in October 1952, tales of Mau Mau savagery spread wildly among white settlers in the colony and at home in Britain. Mau Mau was portrayed as a barbaric, anti-European, and anti-Christian sect that had reverted to tactics of primitive terror to interrupt the British civilizing mission in Kenya."[14] News and images of the purported barbarism spread across Europe and North America next to accounts of the civility of British settlers.[15] In response to the rebellion, the British built a massive network of detention camps, holding between 160,000 to 300,000 Kikuyu insurgents.[16] For the women and children, colonial officials turned roughly eight hundred villages into open-air prisons—complete with barbed wire, watch towers, armed guards, and spiked trenches. According to Elkins, the detention camps and villages meant that the British detained 1.5 million Kikuyus, roughly the entire population.[17]

To cover their tracks, the British would burn some 250,000 files about individual detainees, contriving a balance sheet of violence in which the

Kikuyu possessed the largest expenditures. But as Elkins observes, "Officially, fewer than one hundred Europeans, including settlers, and some eighteen hundred loyalists died at the hands of the Mau Mau."[18] The official British figures say that eleven thousand Kikuyu were killed, but Elkins puts the number higher, saying, "I now believe there was in late colonial Kenya a murderous campaign to eliminate Kikuyu people, a campaign that left tens of thousands, perhaps hundreds of thousands, dead."[19]

There were the men who—upon entering the detention camp—were made to run through a cattle dip with disinfectant. The ones who couldn't swim often died. Someone told of the men who were forced to jump up and down with shackled ankles, leaping until their skin was ripped from their bones. There was the woman who gave birth to her baby, right after the British burned down her house and stole her cattle. Realizing that there were not enough homes for the incarcerated, the British officers sent the women (Young. Old. Barren. Pregnant. It didn't matter) into the forests, ordering them to bring back logs and reeds to build a makeshift village.

Those injustices and cruelties preoccupy Mutu, and she poses a set of questions that are at the center of her work: "How does one talk about cultural decapitation or historical uprooting? How does one capture the moment after a limb has been severed or a Nation's heart has been broken?" Her work implores us to make sense of histories of violence that shape the wounds of our present, and by tracing those lesions, we are not only surveying colonialism's harms but postcolonialism's hurts as well.

The Aftermath of Anti-Colonialism

When independence from colonial rule came to African countries, it dragged into the new day the very violence that many presumed would be left behind. Indeed, as the feminist scholars Amina Mama and Margo Okazawa-Rey argue, "When victory came, and political transitions to African rule came, the institutions of state bore the marks of a patriarchal and militaristic history."[20] The marks could be seen in the ways that newly independent African states tried to restore the masculine prowess that leaders believed colonialism had stolen. This "restoration" would lead to political cultures characterized by "authoritarian and militarist legacies."

One way of interpreting Mutu's art is by seeing it as a response to the postcolonial world created by those political cultures and their effect on women and the environment. We can also read it as an answer to the role that the United States has played in promoting toxic political cultures in the global south. For this reason, her works are filled with wounds. Mutu said that when she came to the United States in the 1990s she began wounding her artwork to produce "a permanent reminder of this inner rage that probably emanated from feeling uncomfortable as a foreigner in the United States in a time of war and xenophobia."[21] Wounding the walls of her pieces was a way of acknowledging her rage about "the [US–Mexico] border, about environmental destruction, [and] about waste and human conflict."[22] Indeed, Mutu's work inspires us to illuminate the connections between forms of state violence across the globe.

Mama and Okazawa-Rey point to the influence that the US and the USSR as the major Cold War superpowers had on African countries. According to them, "During the first decades of independence (1950s–1990s), which overlap with the Cold War era, Africa was caught up in the politics of East versus West. Both sides provided massive military assistance driven by their strategic interests."[23] Hence, independence in Africa was constantly being shaped by the military might of the United States and the Soviet Union, a fact that would frustrate the claims of African leaders that their plans for decolonization were solely autonomous and therefore divorced from Western and Soviet influence.

In many ways, Mutu's work depicts the aftermath of military assistance and the political cultures that this assistance unleashed. In doing so, it demands that we revisit the histories of anti-colonialism in Africa. In fact, her work suggests that patriarchal and militaristic models complicated the histories of anti-colonialism and helped shatter social life in the eras of independence.

Mutu's 2005 piece *Misguided Little Unforgiveable Hierarchies* (figure 25) suggests such an intervention. Similar to *This You Call Civilization?* the piece depicts a woman squatting in tall grass. Another smaller woman with heels stands atop her. This figure is bent over to face the squatting woman. Atop the bent-over figure sits another female figure. It has the legs of a woman but the torso and head of a monkey. The faces of the squatting woman and her bent-over sister are made of cut-outs from magazines. The piece is splotched with blood.

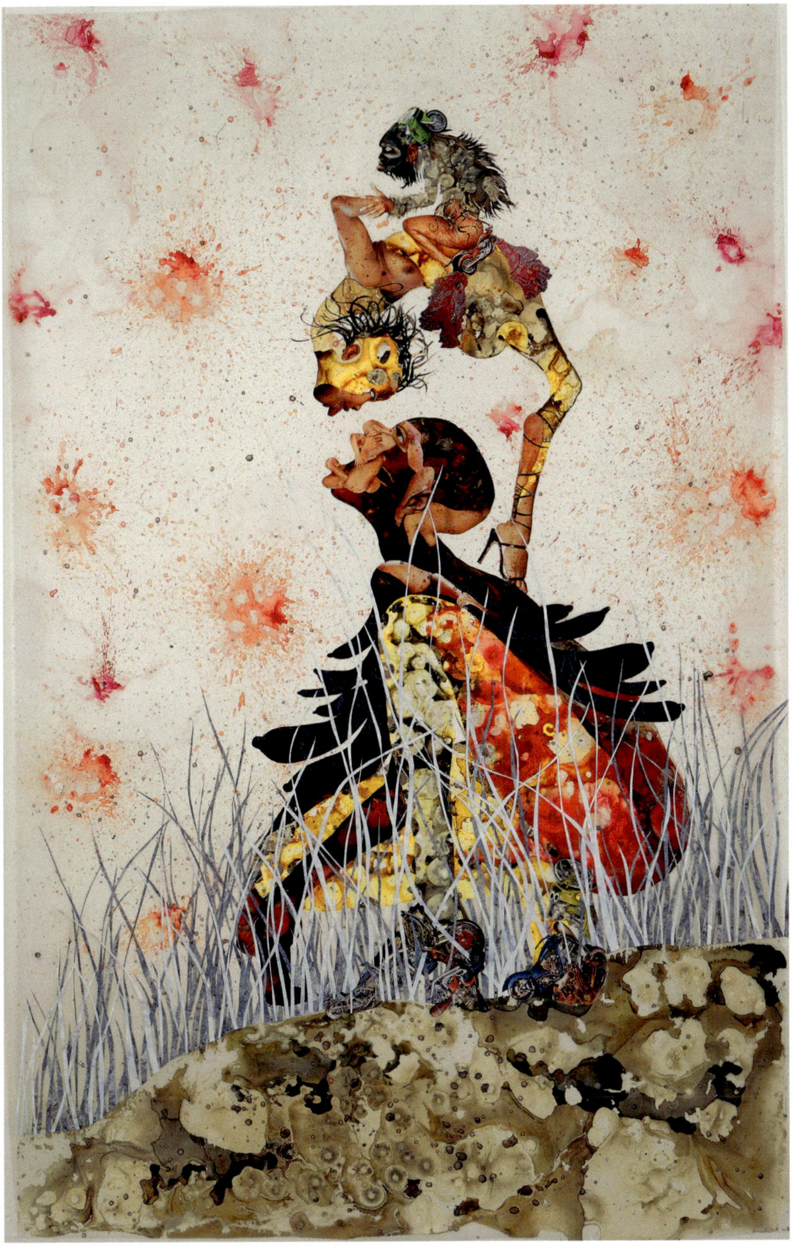

Figure 25. Wangechi Mutu. *Misguided Little Unforgiveable Hierarchies*. 2005. Ink, acrylic, collage, and contact paper on Mylar, 81 x 52 in.

The stacked figures in the piece recall the days of settler colonialism and anti-colonialism. The curator Trevor Schoonmaker implies these histories when he says, "The stacked form is . . . evocative of Makonde sculptures from East Africa, where clusters of interconnected figures represent family trees."[24] In particular, *Misguided Unforgiveable Little Hierarchies* recalls the art produced by the Makonde people during the days of anti-colonial rebellion. In the 1960s, Makonde sculptors were inspired by anti-colonial and socialist struggles, particularly in Tanzania and Mozambique. Makonde carvers in Mozambique were, in fact, supported by the Mozambican nationalist group Front for the Liberation of Mozambique or FRELIMO, which organized cooperatives for the production and global distribution of Makonde sculptures. Through the international market, FRELIMO used Makonde sculptures to build support for independence from the Portuguese.

Indeed, the Ujamaa towers, as they were called, were one of the most popular genres that FRELIMO marketed for international distribution. Made from a single piece of wood, the towers typically depicted groups of interlinked people, standing, crouching, sitting, or hanging (see figure 26). The towers were named after the Kiswahili word for "socialism" and in honor of the Tanganyika African National Union (TANU), the political party that made socialism into its guiding principle and that supported FRELIMO in its efforts at liberation.[25]

A 1962 TANU pamphlet written by Julius K. Nyerere, the leader of TANU and future president of Tanzania, grounded the organization's notion of socialism in ideals of family from African societies and as a critique of Western capitalism and Soviet socialism's thirst for power. This effort to transcend Western capitalism and Soviet socialism would inspire TANU to promote a humanist notion of socialism that exceeded national boundaries. As the pamphlet stated, "Our recognition of the family to which we all belong must be extended yet further—beyond the tribe, the community, the nation, or even the continent—to embrace the whole society of mankind. This is the only logical conclusion for true socialism."[26] The figures depicted in the Ujamaa towers, therefore, are not simply representations of the people in the village but are metaphors for the people of the world.

Whereas the people depicted in the Ujamaa towers expressed the peaceful idealism of Nyerere's theory of African socialism, we can read

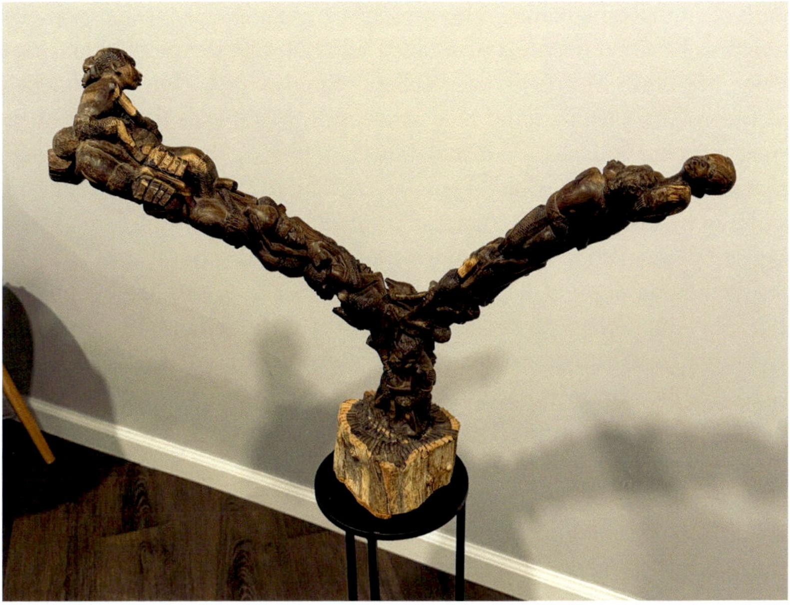

Figure 26. Ujamaa Towers.

Mutu's figures as telling a different and more troubling story, a story that partly involves the colonial contexts that occasioned African socialism in the first place. They point not only to what the Ujamaa towers depicted but what postcolonial independence yielded. For instance, the United States provided military assistance to 94 percent of Africa from 1991 to 1995. By 1998 that assistance amounted to more than $227 million.[27] As this money supported the aims and statuses of dictators and produced political cultures based on patriarchal militarism, military assistance has "posed a formidable obstacle to development and democratization,"[28] as Mama and Okazawa-Rey put it.

Although Mutu's works may invoke the Ujamaa towers, they depart from them in important ways. The Ujamaa towers are made from a single piece of wood, suggesting the oneness of humankind, Mutu's artwork is made of collages, suggesting that humankind is constituted from myriad differences that defy any notion of a universal humanity. Indeed, her figures cross the boundaries of human and nonhuman as they are made up of parts of animals and plants. Whereas the Ujamaa towers depict harmonious relations between people, one cannot help but note the conflict and violence that cover Mutu's figures. As Schoonmaker says, "The red blotches in the collage's background read as wounds; Mutu uses these bloodlike spatters in her collages and installations to reference the violence and war that resulted from the colonial process, particularly that [was] endured and suffered by women."[29] The holes and splotches that dot Mutu's work can hence be understood to be a continent littered with wounds.

The female figures stacked upon each other in pieces like *Misguided Little Unforgiveable Hierarchies* might point to the ways that colonialism and postcolonialism devastated the lives of scores of women. In the context of postcolonial conflicts in Africa, the ratio of casualties in terms of civilians to soldiers is 10:1, whereas it was 1:9 during World War I,[30] a ratio that has made women and children war's foremost victims. *Misguided Little Unforgiveable Hierarchies* depicts, In Schoonmaker's words, "Women's basic and primal bodily functions: birth, sex, and elimination."[31] But it suggests how those basic elements of life are situated in a world elaborated by the atrocities of colonial and postcolonial wars.

The Fruits of War and Militarism

Although the cruelties of history are undoubtable on Mutu's works, there is a pluckiness in her disfigured beauties.[32] As she says, "The bodies in my work are often wracked with the wounds of war and keep on despite missing or twisted limbs." One example is a collage called *Forbidden Fruit Picker* (figure 27). The piece is an obvious rendering of Eve from the Bible. This Eve, though, is drawn according to the conventions that we have come to associate with Mutu. Part of this Eve's leg is amputated; her body is made up of inorganic elements as well as parts from other species. This Eve is reaching for a fruit from a tree that she is sitting under, and two serpents are flicking their tongues at her and her fruit. Despite its nods to the biblical tale, there is nothing idyllic about this portrait, nothing Eden-like; indeed this Eden has already been devastated before Eve even spots the tree. In fact, the telltale signs of war are there—an amputated leg, a blood-stained ground, signs that suggest that war will creep even into the hallowed place.

For most anti-colonial movements, there could be no anti-colonial awakening without war and militarism—"the veneration of military order,

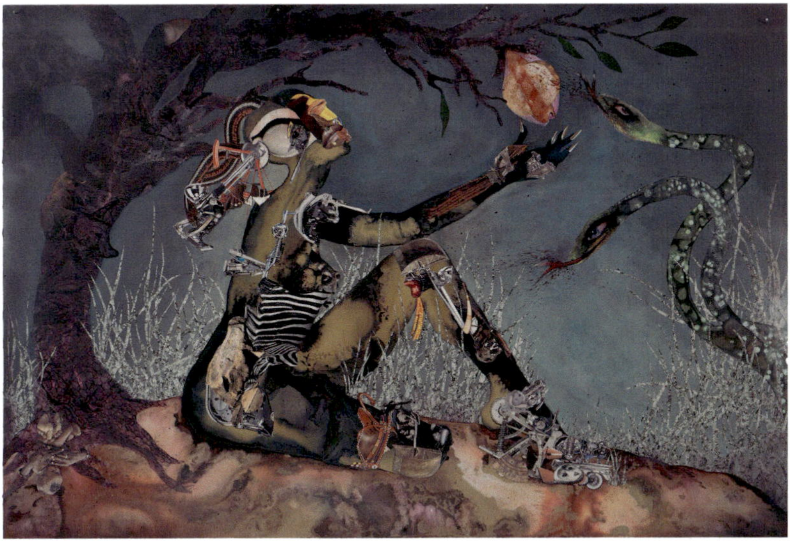

Figure 27. Wangechi Mutu. *Forbidden Fruit Picker.* 2015. Photo montage from printed sources, collage, spray paint, and cut fabric with ink on Mylar and paper board. 39¼ x 58½ in.

accoutrements, and culture."[33] Indeed, Frantz Fanon argued in *The Wretched of the Earth* that the revolutionary politics of anti-colonial fighters are "the essence of the fight which explodes the old colonial truths and reveals unexpected facets."[34] For Fanon, revolutionary violence against colonialism was a means of getting at social and historical truths. As he stated, "Violence alone, violence committed by the people, violence organized and educated by its leaders, makes it possible for the masses to understand social truths and gives the key to them."[35] Though Fanon's regard for violence was not uncritical, *The Wretched of the Earth* understood violence to be the basis for overturning the colonial order and as the means to achieve social and historical clarity.

This view was corroborated by Jean-Paul Sartre's foreword to the book. In it, Sartre castigated the white liberals who believed the guerrilla fighters had gone too far in their quest against colonialism, writing, "They would do well to read Fanon; for he shows clearly that this irrepressible violence is neither sound and fury, nor the resurrection of savage instincts, nor even the effect of resentment: it is man recreating himself." For the colonized, he offered this interpretation: "You may fear or be feared; that is to say, abandon yourself to the disassociations of a sham existence or conquer your birthright of unity. When the peasant takes a gun in his hands, the old myths grow dim, and the prohibitions are one by one forgotten. The rebel's weapon is the proof of his humanity." Weapons will not only aid the struggle for freedom. They can fundamentally usher in a new consciousness and a renewed sense of being.

Writing that "decolonization is always a violent phenomenon,"[36] Fanon—in concert with Sartre—argued for its transformative effects. Fanon said, "[Decolonization] transforms spectators crushed with their inessentiality into privileged actors, with the grandiose glare of history's floodlights upon them." He went on to say, "[Decolonization] brings a natural rhythm into existence, introduced by new men, and with it a new language and a new humanity."[37] Like Sartre, Fanon understood decolonization as putting violence to good psychological and social use.

But *Forbidden Fruit Picker* powerfully rebuts this presumption that war and militarism would lead to human and social betterment. Mutu's Eve is an amputee, and her body has been assembled from various parts. If we read *Forbidden Fruit Picker* in relation to militarization, it serves as a warning. Discussing militarization's impact on Africa, Mama and Okazawa-Rey argue, "The plethora of conflicts that have taken place in postcolonial Africa and the high political, economic, and cultural costs of military rule provide good grounds for arguing that African militarism has generated more insecurity than security, often terrorizing rather than protecting local populations, dominating the political sphere, blurring the boundaries between civilian and military, and thereby undermining all non-military forms of political and institutional authority and accountability."[38] In fact, the image that *Forbidden Fruit Picker* projects is one in which the erstwhile nonmilitarized space of Eden has been ravaged by militarization, a corruption that the snakes have hissed into being.

As *Forbidden Fruit Picker* focuses on what war and militarism have done to the female body, it highlights an area that Fanon neglected. In Aaronette White's assessment of the role that war has played on the social and psychological realities of African men and women, the late scholar argued, "In contrast to Fanon's claims about revolutionary violence as a 'cleansing force,' war is a dirty business and a gendered business."[39] We might understand postcolonial conflicts partly as the legacy of that violence. Postcolonial conflicts have, in the words of Mama and Okazawa-Rey, been characterized by "horrific sexual violence—the widespread and systematic rape and assault of women and girls—along with the mutilation and massacre of civilians."[40] As Mama and Okazawa-Rey observe, "Militarism polarized gender relations and identities, and particular notions of masculinity and masculine prowess seemed to be bound-up with gender violence, which threatens women's security."[41] Rather than militarism protecting the integrity of the home and womanhood, it exposed people's lives, in general, and women's lives, in particular, to new levels of precarity.

Forbidden Fruit Picker also points to the ways that war and militarism snuck into rural spaces. The central figure sits under a tree in a field with native grasses. The bucolic scene is interrupted by snakes and the evidence of amputation. In many ways it symbolizes the consequential place that the rural held in anti-colonial discourse. For Nyerere and TANU, the village was imagined as the place that would allow Tanzanian men, especially, to return to the beneficial effects of agricultural labor and distance them "from the corrupting influences of Western popular culture and urban anomie."[42]

The rural, in TANU's case, was imagined as the site for developing properly gendered men and women. At a youth rally in 1968 at the National Stadium, Nyerere "held up the jembe, or hoe, alongside the gun, as the symbol of young Tanzanian manhood, invoking a pairing common in African socialism."[43] Discussing socialist Tanganyika's investment in gender and sexual norms, the historian Priya Lal notes, "Concerns about the organization and reproduction of African families were at the heart of late colonial development policy in Tanganyika, as across British Africa."[44] TANU extended those concerns and made them part of socialist and revolutionary policies. As Lal argues, TANU'S "official anxieties . . . fixated on unmarried, mobile urban women, who were consistently rendered as prostitutes and incarnations of moral decay."[45] For TANU, the village was imagined as a site that would recover the gender and sexual integrity of African communities and would fulfill a militarized vision of African communities as well, but as *Forbidden Fruit Picker* suggests, this vision would lead to all kinds of devastation. To this end, there are women who can tell you of how postcolonial conflict upended their lives and those of the people around them—women who made their way from farm to farm in search of food, women who hid their produce from soldiers, women who made salt from boiled sea water, and women who became the "companions" of soldiers, waiting for the day that war would end.

Like *Forbidden Fruit Picker,* these images reproach the presumption that war will yield a cleaner life and society. Addressing Fanon's belief in that presumption, White argues, "In addition to justifying violence as a means of physical self-defense for the colonized, Fanon attributed a therapeutic, psychological role to revolutionary war. The question today becomes therapeutic for whom and in what way?"[46] Reflecting on the nature of war, White continues by saying, "The patriarchal nature of war, militarism, and military training appear to perpetuate the violent injustices and entrench the colonized masculinities Fanon predicted they would eradicate."[47] Perpetuating the violence and entrenching the masculinities honed in colonialism may explain, as White puts it, "why some of the most visionary revolutionary organizations and their leaders have over time come to mimic the authoritarian, elitist, and violent characteristics of the regimes they overthrew."[48]

It's important, though, not to read Mutu's fruit picker or the African women who have survived war and conflict as history's victims. Women on the continent fought in the anti-colonial wars and have organized brilliantly in the name of peace. If we look at the fruit picker as a symbol of those women, we might say that she is far from the image of the retiring victim. Her non-amputated leg sports a high-heeled shoe made of auto parts and an African mask, and the hand that reaches for the fruit is bedecked in manicured nails.

Rather than depicting her as the biblical ingenue, Mutu casts her Eve as having already experienced the worst that the world has to offer. Instead of expressing hesitancy, as the classical Eve did, this Eve exudes a self-possession amid the obvious signs of historical trauma. She is the woman who emerged after the loss of innocence rather than the one who brought that loss about. As opposed to bringing evil into the world, evil picked this Eve long before she picked the fruit.

The Eve in *Forbidden Fruit Picker* is the sister to the Eve in Mutu's 2010 piece *Root of All Eves.* That piece depicts Eve open-mouthed with sunglasses and one severed arm, the stump of which is bloodied. She sits cross-legged and is made of organic and inorganic parts, held up by another female figure who is rooted beneath the surface of a mangrove. About the 2010 Eve's assuredness, the critic and theorist Jillian Hernandez says, "Here Eve, whose transgression in the Garden of Eden has been framed as the cause of women's moral downfall and sexual deviancy, holds court."[49] Like *The Root of All Eves*, *Forbidden Fruit Picker* presents an Eve who suggests a self-determination that is inseparable from her disfigurement and her sensuality. The Fruit Picker casts aside any notion that the circumstances of war have crushed African women into the ground of victimhood. With all the confidence that manicured nails and a parted-mouth suggest, this grown woman—tried and tested by war—claims her fruit as well as her appetites.

Just Wars and the Problem of Patriarchy

Mutu's work compels us to consider the ways that war has made us who we are. Whether colonial or postcolonial, war has produced the most terrible forms of human agency. It has caused us to measure our strength in terms of all the ways in which we can burn, break, cut, shoot, poison, wound, and explode. Read as a meditation on violence, Mutu's work begs us to reconsider the murderous capacities that war produces.

Michel Foucault analyzed how war remakes human beings by enticing them with abilities they never thought they could achieve. The late eighteenth century, he said, was the period in which the young man who first possessed the appearance of the peasant could—through training and discipline—later don the air of the soldier. The soldier learns how to control his body and wield his weapons (which include his body) for the purposes of war. Defining the docile soldier not in terms of meekness but according to the soldier's capacity to be "used, transformed, and improved,"[50] Foucault summed up the late eighteenth century by saying, "The soldier has become something that can be made."[51] And with that Foucault suggests that militarism is one of the means for subjecting us to dominant forms of power; it subjects us, though, not by breaking us down but by building us up.

War and militarism—the processes that have built some up—are the reasons that others have been broken down, as Mutu's work suggests. Even more, Mutu's work urges us to reconsider how those traditions have invested in militaristic models of human agency as well. As our discussion of Fanon and other revolutionaries shows, Black liberation has used war to imagine a renewed sense of human agency. Discussing the role of war in African American liberation, Jennifer James argues, for instance, "African Americans have turned to the language of war and warfare to conceptualize black struggle against a racialized state."[52] In fact, from the abolition of slavery to the struggles against racial segregation, war has been the organizing metaphor for struggles against anti-Black racism within the United States. As a result, war has provided much of the foundation for how we think of African American agency.

But as frameworks for being in the world, militaristic models—even when women have taken up arms—have refortified forms of patriarchy. As Amina Mama argues, "Militarism clearly propagated masculine ideals that were based on the capacity to kill as much as on the capacity to commandeer national resources, and which excluded the vast majority of men as well as women from this monopoly."[53] To the extent that they invested in those models, liberation struggles have inherited and extended patriarchal notions of agency. According to one former girl combatant for FRELIMO or the Liberation Front of Mozambique, during the civil war which lasted from 1976 to 1992, "[In] 1975, FRELIMO began recruiting and abducting girls into their forces.'"[54] This former soldier added, "'FRELIMO recruiters with buses arrived at schools asked girls to volunteer for the military; when few volunteered, a number of girls were rounded up and forced onto the buses, despite protests from the teachers and the girls. This process was repeated at a number of schools until the buses were full.'"[55] Another girl soldier for the Ugandan National Resistance Army recounted experiences of how female soldiers were also forced to provide sexual services for male officers: "We female soldiers had to offer sex to more than five officers in one unit. Nearly every evening an officer would order you to report to his place, usually 9pm."[56]

In her discussion of gender and sexual politics among the Mau Mau, the historian Tabitha Kanogo writes,

> In certain camps, male leaders were each allowed to choose a woman . . . who as well as seeing to the other needs of the leader was also expected to meet his sexual needs. Women were induced to fulfill such "tasks" for "the good of the cause." As one Mau Mau woman stated, "Generally, I would think of sleeping

> with a man as an individual concern. Here, it seems to me that the leaders consider this as part of the woman's duty in [Mau Mau] society. I believe that since I could not do any other better to my people, I would then willingly accept it as my contribution to society."

With FRELIMO and the Mau Mau, we can see how the just rebellion against colonialism required gender inequality and sexual domination. Colonial violence made anti-colonial violence the likely option, but did this choice necessitate gender and sexual violence?

Popularizing the notion that liberation struggles produce just wars, Lenin said, "[We] fully recognize the justice, the progressivism and the necessity of civil wars, i.e. wars of an oppressed class against the oppressor, of slaves against the slave-holders, of serfs against the landowners, of wage-workers against the bourgeoisie."[57] But wars—even the ones with progressive motivations—can lead to historic betrayals and violations. In the case of Africa, White notes, "Contemporary postcolonial civil wars in Africa are more complex and difficult to identify as 'just wars.'"[58] Even when those wars started with just motivations, those motivations, as White says, "often disappear,"[59] as the civil wars in Liberia, Sierra Leone, Somalia, Ethiopia, Eritrea, and other countries have shown. Former allies become enemies, and the lust for money and power produces "an entirely new generation of warlords."[60] Just wars often rely on the same principles as their unjust counterparts. As White says, "The values needed for effective warfare (violence, authoritarianism, elitism, secrecy and tight control of information for fear of spies and leaks) contradict the values needed for effective revolutionary transformation (egalitarianism, freedom of expression, consensus, dissent, transparency in government decisions and policies)."[61] These histories and Mutu's work urge us to ask, "Under what conditions can war fulfill radical visions for human agency and social justice?"

The Beautiful Monstrosity of Fusions

The art historian Kristine Stiles argues that Wangechi Mutu's work "fuses the history of colonialism, and its iconographic shards of Diaspora, displacement, migration, and globalization, with images of cybernetic, post-biological, hyphenated, black, brown, and white bodies."[62] While Mutu's collages suggest that humans, animals, technology, and plants came together as a result of historical violence, the work poses the question of how this terrible convergence might inspire new and productive relations between them.

In her 2002 *Riding Death in My Sleep* (figure 28), Mutu depicts a female figure crouched atop a mound covered in mushrooms. A bald eagle's head with talons but no torso stands to her right. The figure wears a body that, as the art critic Holland Cotter describes it, is "patterned to look at once bejeweled, reptilian, and diseased."[63] She also sports high-heeled boots, the calves of which are ornamented with raffia from the palm tree native to Africa. Mutu has also patterned the suit to look as if it is part of the figure's skin. A creature that is part insect and part lizard crawls on her shoulder; a reptile-elephant-bird flies close to her head. In this figure's world, insects, humans, plants, and animals are curiously recomposed and integrated. Judging from the title, the merger between life forms has taken place through death and its surroundings.

And if the title is any judge, all the creatures—the cat, the butterfly, the eagle with no body, the woman made of earth and animals, even the mushrooms—all of them bear witness to the catastrophe that war has left behind. Indeed, we are accustomed to thinking of war as something that primarily affects human beings, but, in fact, it devastates all forms of life. In a 2020 report, the environmental and humanitarian organization Conflict and Environment Observatory (CEOBS) suggests that war jeopardizes multiple forms of life. About the environment, CEOBS argues, "The environmental impact of wars begins long before they do. Building and sustaining military forces consumes vast quantities of resources."[64] The environment becomes the stage upon which to violently develop and exercise human agency. As the organization says, "Maintaining military readiness means training, and training consumes resources."[65] In addition, militarism endangers land and water resources. "Weapons and military material used during conflicts,"[66] according to CEOBS, "also leave environmental legacies. Land mines, cluster munitions and other explosive remnants of war can restrict access to agricultural land and pollute soils and water sources with metals and toxic energetic materials."[67] Militarism fundamentally jeopardizes the integrity of the natural world.

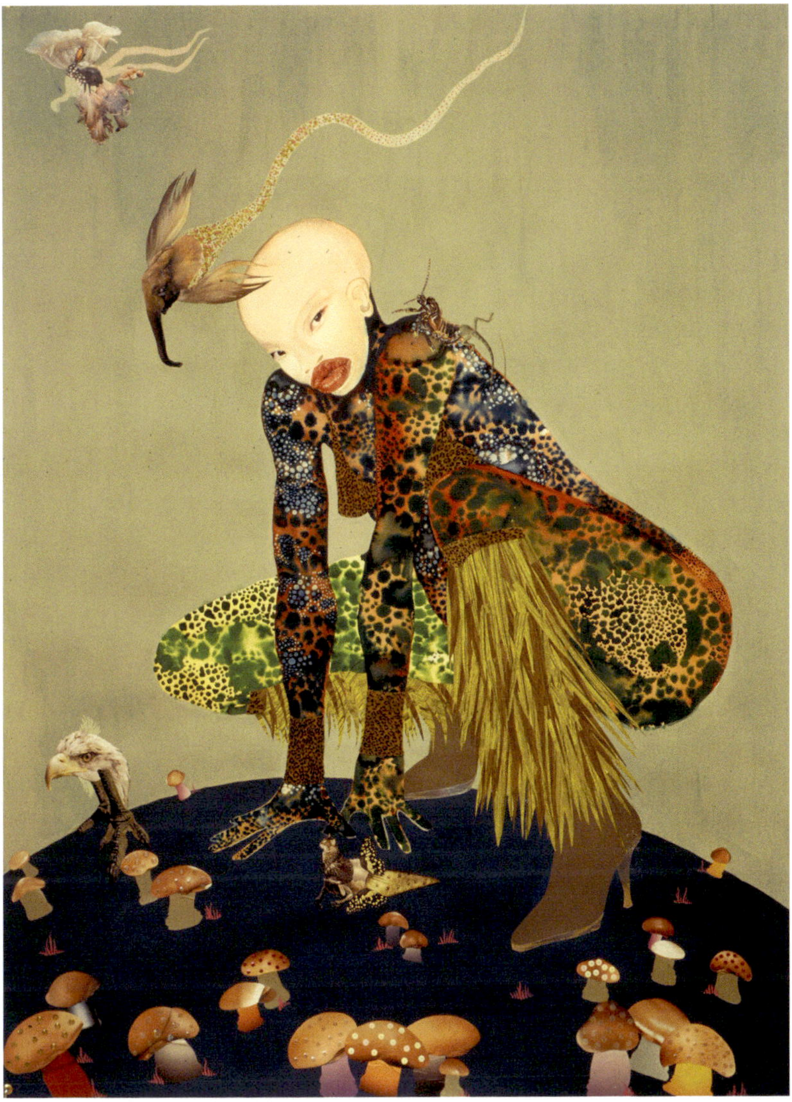

Figure 28. Wangechi Mutu. *Riding Death in My Sleep*. 2002. Ink and collage on paper, 60 x 44 in.

Militarism also presents specific dangers to wildlife. CEOBS notes how animals are put at risk merely in the build-up of military forces, writing, "Easy access to small arms and light weapons can harm wildlife through facilitating increased hunting and poaching, and the ungoverned spaces created by conflict create the ideal spaces for wildlife crime."[68] Increased military presence can also lead to environmental disorder as vehicles, fences, walls, and training areas disrupt wildlife. If war has made it such that "we no longer live in nature,"[69] as James argues, and "we are positioned in a struggle against it,"[70] then we must count the diverse makeup of nature as part of war's fatalities.

Replete with images of a ravaged earth, Mutu's art implies that war and militarism give birth to many ruins. This revelation—that war represents the dangerous enhancement of human capacity and constitutes the perilous degradation of all forms of life—is a devastating wake-up call for Black radical traditions. As those liberation movements failed to consider the environment, they facilitated the environment's destruction in anti-colonial and postcolonial conflicts. The Prussian general and military theorist Carl von Clausewitz argued that "war was nothing but a duel on a larger scale."[71] Jennifer James, in her interpretation, reads him as designating war as a "contest between two people—a 'self' and an 'other.'" That contest, she goes on to say, is "enlarged into a conflict between multiple 'selves' (the same as you) and multiple 'others' (different from you but indistinct from one another)."[72] But contemporary wars and conflicts have multiplied the "others" that must contend with those wars and conflicts. In addition to various types of peoples, contemporary wars and conflicts involve water, land, plants, insects, and animals. These various others are suggested in *Riding Death in My Sleep*. If we read the piece as a meditation on war and militarism, it implies all the assorted others that war has brought into relation.

Like the other works discussed in this book, Mutu's art compels a reimagined Black radical tradition. It does so in several ways. Her work calls us to challenge forms of colonial domination to be sure, but it also compels us to challenge certain visions of anti-colonialism as well. While the latter has called for greater distributions of wealth and the abolition of racial, colonial, and capitalist hierarchies, they have also been guilty of investing in the very patriarchal systems and ideologies that have constituted racist and colonial societies.

In addition, Mutu's work demands a wholesale reckoning with war and militarism. Instead of imagining them as battles between patriarchs, her art emerges from a long historical period in which war devastates civilians, particularly women and children, much more than soldiers. Her work calls for a Black radicalism that can bear witness to the social and gendered violence of war and militarism. For Black radical traditions this would mean a questioning of war and militarism as a means of producing just transformations. This involves a thorough critique of the taken-for-granted blueprints for being and moving in the world. In Mutu's collages, war and militarism—even in their "just" modes—are not life's simple enhancements but often its devastating alterations.

There is a shocking and unpredictable beauty in Mutu's work. It is the pieced-together beauty of new associations between the human and the other forms of matter on our planet. In her imagination, war's devastation of human and natural worlds can be the basis of fantastic new relations and alliances between those domains. Like the collages that she creates, our lives can be ones in which the inorganic and the organic, the human and the more-than-human, the animal and the botanical can achieve a new fraternity. There is a wisdom in this observance. Ruin can be the seedbed of wonder.

We might also think of Mutu's pieces as reviving a signature aspect of Black radical traditions—the refusal to take Africa as an abstraction and instead engage it for the living and complex formation that it is. Mutu's collages are composed of so many parts that they compel the viewer to peer closely at them to decipher all that is there. We might take this as a metaphor for how we should look at Africa as well—as an entity composed of countless intricacies, ones that are irreducible to a single element. This is also a way of saying that we must acknowledge that Blackness lives in more places than the United States and that we must attend to the lives of Blackness across a variety of regions and histories, each one constituted by their own astonishing layers. And if we listen and peer closely, the figures might begin to volunteer their story:

It's hard to tell how many parts we are.
We are leaves, rhizomes, and leopard skins.
We are motorcycles
and women who were raped every evening at 9.

We are the former sex-worker-soldiers
who crouch in the grass that once was our mattress.
We are the workers who built the prisons that the colonizers
    threw us in.
We are the leftovers of war.
Our flesh has turned into a glow of colors.
We have made our bodies into
schools for
walking,
flying,
crawling,
creeping,
and growing things.
One day
they will arise
as the true faces of freedom.
We are the mix of worlds.[7]

Conclusion

To Make Things Happen

The African American artist Cauleen Smith was clear about the stakes of her 2017 installation *Human__3.0. Reading List.* In fact, the installation was dreamt in response to anti-Black violence, neoliberalism, and privatization. By the time it debuted, Tanisha Anderson, Michael Brown, Philando Castile, Miriam Carey, Michelle Cusseaux, Shelly Frey, Korryn Gaines, Eric Garner, India Kager, Trayvon Martin, Tamir Rice, Walter Scott, Alton Sterling, and many other Black people had been murdered by the police, had died in their custody, or were killed by vigilantes who claimed the police's authority.[1]

In addition to these killings, political and economic realities in the United States had grown more dire in the years leading up to Smith's installation. In 2010 the US Supreme Court in *Citizens United v. Federal Elections Commission* ruled that corporations had the rights of individuals in terms of both speech and spending, a decision that increased the power of the wealthy to mold elections from the shadows. And in 2017, public entities such as streets, schooling, water, and even democracy were turned into the knickknacks of the market.[2]

Out of an awareness of these crises, Smith drew by hand fifty-seven book covers of texts that she said "literally changed my life, sustained my life, but also (fair warning) make it difficult for me to go along, get along, look the other way and gets mines."[3] The drawings include the covers of Octavia Butler's *Wild Seed*, W. E. B. Du Bois's *The World and Africa*,

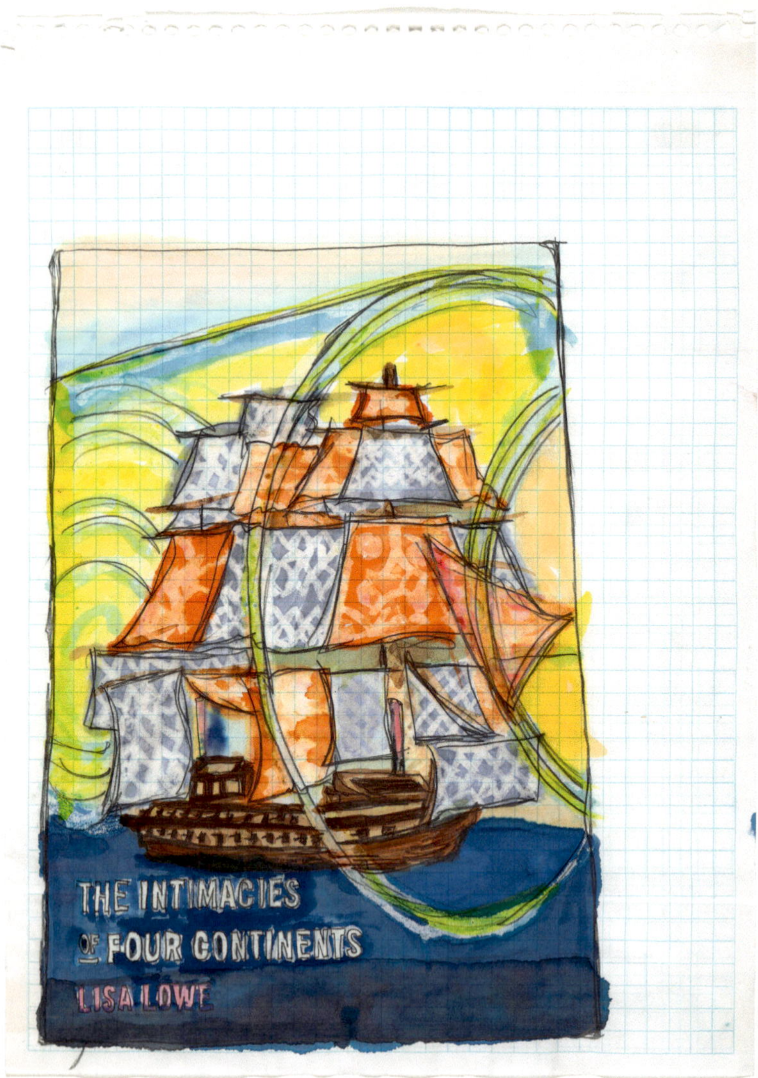

Figure 29. Cauleen Smith. *Lisa Lowe, The Intimacies of Four Continents*. From *Human_3.0 Reading List*. 2015. 30 x 21.5 cm (11 13/16 x 8 1/2 in.) Art Institute of Chicago, Chicago. Reprinted with permission.

Frantz Fanon's *Black Skin, White Masks*, Lisa Lowe's *The Intimacies of Four Continents*, Fred Moten's *In the Break: The Aesthetics of the Black Radical Tradition*, Cedric Robinson's *Black Marxism: The Making of the Black Radical Tradition*, and Donna Haraway's *Simians, Cyborgs, and Nature: The Reinvention of Nature.*

By drawing books that she wanted people to read, Smith wasn't simply trying to make the texts pleasing to the eye. She was turning our attention to publications that can assist us in changing the world. As she said, "I wanted these books to be noticed, and, in our photo-saturated world, drawing them slowed people down and invited renewed interest. One thing I can offer young people is information on how to use language to affect change."[4] Smith used her hand to leverage imagery for the good of literacy and social transformation.

The art historian Susan Owens tells us that many millennia ago, ancient people used earth pigments such as ochre, sienna, and umber to draw animals, hunters, and rocks on the walls of caves. Whether they drew things for worship, magic, or commemoration, "What seems certain," she says, "is the images were made for communities to forge connections with the world and its creatures, literally to inscribe themselves and their stories into the land."[5] Smith assumed this time-honored practice and drew texts whose ideas and questions could be engraved on the spaces around them.

In offering language and images as means of affecting change, Smith was activating drawing's capacity to be "an engine room of creation."[6] We might say that the exhibition implied the concept of àshe. If this ancient belief denotes the capacity to make things happen, the drawings suggest our ability to change history rather than merely inherit it. Indeed, the images of the various book covers imply that—pencil in hand—we can draw our way into other forms of being. In other words, to truly know these radical books, we must try to live them out.

Marxist philosophy defines this union of knowledge and action as praxis. Describing it, the Hungarian theorist Georg Lukács said, "Action, praxis—which Marx demanded before all else in his *Theses on Feuerbach*—is in essence the penetration and transformation of reality."[7] Transforming reality can only take place through critical consciousness. Noting this, Lukács argued, "[Only] the unity of theory and practice can provide a real basis for social revolution and the total transformation of society."[8]

Marxist philosophy has always understood the transformation of the given social order as a vital form of labor. As the theorists Michael Hardt and Antonio Negri argued, "Living labor is the internal force that constantly poses not only the subversion of the capitalist process of production but also the construction of the alternative."[9] *Human 3.0* steps into this critical tradition as it draws book covers that act as pictographs of critical knowledge and social change.

As her manifesto shows, Smith is keenly aware of the obstacles that inhibit the acquisition of understanding and the fulfillment of just societies. A powerful impediment, according to her, is neoliberalism. Using the concept to discuss the transfer of wealth from producers to profiteers, she says, "Neoliberalism, for which the *Human__3.0 Reading List* is a low-grade inoculation, turns our communities into markets, into auction blacks—I mean auction blocks."[10] As neoliberalism transforms our towns and cities into places that exist less for us and more for corporations, it veers toward those days of slavery in which human life did not live for its own sake but for the good of power. To understand these processes and to defy them, we need that knowledge distilled from critical traditions, those texts and artworks that point us toward oppositional literacy and action.

This movement from imagery to information is expressed in the history of drawing. As Owens notes, for instance, "Drawing itself begins with the telling of stories."[11] Its maneuvers are also conveyed in *Human__3.0*. As artists thousands of years ago drew stories involving deer, horses, bulls, and bison, Smith drew books whose stories can explain the ins and outs of our human drama. Her drawings begin with the stories of how radical traditions are invested in literature and art as ways to meet the world.

Indeed, the record of Black radicalism is filled with histories of the enlightening powers of literature and visual art. When he was thirteen years old, Frederick Douglass—forlorn, enslaved, but literate—discovered a book titled *The Columbian Orator.* Burdened not only by slavery but by the notion that he would be a "slave for life,"[12] he found that the book inspired him to emerge from his sorrows. About the book's speeches, he said, "I got a bold and powerful denunciation of oppression and a most brilliant vindication of the rights of man. Here indeed was a noble acquisition. If I had ever wavered under the consideration that the Almighty, in some way, had ordained slavery and willed my enslavement for His own glory, I wavered no longer."[13] Noting that the book illuminated a deeper historical truth, he said, "I had now penetrated to the secret of all slavery and all oppression and had ascertained their true foundation to be in the pride, the power, and the avarice of man."[14]

Similarly, Malcolm X came to literature while incarcerated at Norfolk Prison Colony in Massachusetts. In the prison's fabled library, he read authors such as H. G. Wells, W. E. B. Du Bois, and Carter G. Woodson and studied the histories of African and Chinese civilizations. About his voracious intellectual appetite, he said, "No university would ask any student to devour literature as I did when this new world opened to me, of being able to read and understand."[15]

In addition, the Black gay writer Joseph Beam said of his discovery of lesbian feminist writings—particularly those by women of color, "I was fed by Audre Lorde's *Zami*, Barbara Smith's *Home Girls*, Cherrie Moraga's *Loving in the War Years*, Barbara Deming's *We Cannot Live without Our Lives*, June Jordan's *Civil Wars*, and Michelle Cliff's *Claiming an Identity They Taught Me to Despise*."[16] Naming the impact that this work had on his inner life, he went on to say, "Their courage told me that I, too, could be courageous. I, too, could not only live with what I feel, but could draw succor from it, nurture it, and make it visible."[17]

Discussing the impact of Zora Neale Hurston's 1937 novel *Their Eyes Were Watching God*, the Black feminist scholar Mary Helen Washington wrote, "[For] most black women readers discovering *Their Eyes* for the first time, what was most compelling was the figure of Janie Crawford—powerful, articulate, self-reliant and radically different from any woman character they had ever before encountered in literature."[18] Washington underlined the necessity of "[remembering] the history that nurtured this text into rebirth, especially the collective spirit of the sixties and seventies that galvanized us into political action to retrieve the lost works of black women writers."[19]

Visual work has had a similar function in Black radicalism. It has revealed the contradictions and traps of a society. It has inspired action against historical snares. And it has often provided designs for how people can produce other forms of community. For instance, the Chicago-based artists' collective AfriCOBRA (African Commune for Bad Relevant Artists) believed in making art for Black communities—art that was accessible and that "shined."[20] AfriCOBRA member Jeff Donaldson wrote in the group's 1968 manifesto *Ten in Search of a Nation*, for instance, "This is 'poster art'—images that deal with concepts that offer positive and feasible solutions to our individual, local, national, international, and cosmic problems."[21] For AfriCOBRA and many other Black artists, Black art was necessarily interventionist.

It's important to note that this politicized conception of Black art would exceed national boundaries. In 1979, for instance, a group of Black British artists formed the BLK Art Group. Announcing their 1984 convention "Radical Black Art: A Working Convention," they wrote, "This convention was organized by the BLK ART GROUP, an association of young black artists and art students, who share a common commitment to the development of an art which responds directly to the social and political conditions faced by black people worldwide." [22]

Samella Lewis, a pioneering African American artist and art historian, wrote in her monumental text, *African American Art and Artists*, first printed in 1978: "A primary obligation of African American artists is to understand and use, whenever possible, elements of their cultural heritage. A second obligation is to understand the power of art and the use of that power to inform and to educate."[23] Although many Black artists might disagree with this sentiment, it demonstrates a widely held belief at the time that making Black art meant immersing oneself in Black culture. Lewis's mentor Elizabeth Catlett also believed that a truly accomplished visual literacy meant learning about the visual works produced by Black and other marginalized peoples. Catlett said, "Culture can be a beginning for our involvement with other peoples who share with us racial or national discrimination and exploitation by a common enemy."[24] Emphasizing a relational and coalitional politics, she said, "Today it is difficult to wrap ourselves in 'Blackness,' ignoring the rest of exploited humanity, for we are an integral part of it. Blackness is important as a part of the struggle—it is our part—not only of Blacks in the US, Africa, and the Caribbean, but of Chicanos and Puerto Ricans in the US, and the peoples of Asia and Latin America exemplified at the moment by the Chileans and the Vietnamese."[25]

For Catlett, art was a workshop for developing common cause against oppressive forces. As she said, "Through art we can bring understanding to Black America, Chicano America, Puerto Rican America, etc. of the character of racism, the need for its elimination, our mutual problems, and our differences."[26] For her and Lewis, art could be a means of facing the world with a new kind of worldliness.

For Black radical artists and intellectuals, literary and visual works have often been ways of getting at the historical causes of inequality. They have been means of linking political consciousness to cultural knowledge. They have served as routes for developing an understanding of how the local, the national, and the global come together. They have been ways of seeing how Black struggles are linked to the struggles of other peoples. In sum, they have been powerful resources for getting people to see anew. Indeed, the great lesson of Black critical literature and art has been the steadfast observation that perceiving differently is the requirement for acting otherwise. This is the indispensable precondition for all social change.

With this observation in mind, Smith worries about those intellectual currents that can suspend transformation. "Naw, this ain't no Afro-pessimism shit,"[27] she says. "This reading list is for the Doers-who-Think; not the academics who think there's no point."[28] As an intellectual formation, Afro-pessimism has achieved considerable power within and outside colleges and universities. It has provided many people with a language for talking about the pervasiveness of anti-Blackness in the social world. Indeed, in a period in which Black people are violated routinely by racist forces, we cannot underestimate the importance of having frameworks that can give shape to our outcries. But while Afro-pessimism can often identify violence, it presently lacks a political agenda for addressing it.

In his article "Afro-pessimism and the End of Redemption," Frank Wilderson III—one of Afro-pessimism's originators—presents Afro-pessimism as a formation that recoils from political engagement. He writes, for instance, "In its critique of social movements, Afro-Pessimism argues that Blacks do not function as political subjects; instead, our flesh and energies are instrumentalized for postcolonial, immigrant, feminist, LGBT, and workers' agendas."[29] With this, Wilderson suggests that Black people have simply been the tools of other groups' political movements. Part of what's curious about this formulation is that there is no acknowledgment of the political struggles that Black people have created over hundreds of years. Indeed, as the quote indicates, the article presents Black people as entities without historical and political agency.

We can locate this construction within the essay's argument that Afro-pessimism is founded on a simple equation: *Blackness = slavery*. Wilderson puts it this way: "Afro-Pessimism is premised on an iconoclastic claim: that Blackness is coterminous with Slaveness. Blackness is social death, which is to say that there was never a prior meta-moment of plenitude, never a moment of equilibrium, never a moment of social life."[30] By equating Blackness with social death, Wilderson insinuates that Blackness and in fact Black people are incapable of life's agencies—creating communities, sustaining relationships, generating happiness, and so on. Since Black people are not (and have never been apparently) political agents, the relationships that we have evolved over hundreds of years in local, national, and international struggles are as bogus as fool's gold. And if Blackness has simply been the tool of other groups, it has only ever been in the service of categories that presumably have nothing to do with us—categories such as "gender," "sexuality," "disability, "postcolonialism," "labor." Hard, unyielding, and nonrelational, Blackness stands off from other forms of difference, telling itself that it is not already composed of the very differences it spurns.

On careful inspection though, we see that this Afro-pessimist declaration clashes even with the theorists credited with its birth. One of the concept's inspirations is the Jamaican writer and theorist Sylvia Wynter. In her article "On Disenchanting Discourse: 'Minority' Literary Criticism and Beyond," she argues that the nineteenth century fostered Western Man as a political and intellectual ideal and then presented the native other as Man's antithesis, establishing the other as the boogeyman of "bourgeois-occidental rationality"[31] and "metaphysical Being."[32] Hence, the dominant Western episteme tried to construct the Native other as a wholly irrational being whose life was nonsensical as far as Western norms were concerned. Because of this, Wynter warns against "taking the ontological 'facts' of class and race as if they were brute facts."[33] To do so would be to remain "trapped in the context and code of the hegemonic order."[34] As Afro-pessimism equates Blackness with enslavement, it becomes enchanted by the dominant logic.

In addition to convincing people that what it says about the other is true, Western Man also tries to persuade us that various social forces are unrelated. Critiquing this, Wynter argues against "[overlooking] the reciprocally reinforcing systemic function of 'class' and 'race' and indeed of gender and sexuality."[35] Challenging the separation of social differences is, for her, essential to forming alliances across those categories. Banding together, Western Man's others can transform "the present episteme and its now objectified mode of rationalistic knowledge"[36] and refute an authority that says to be the other is to be a slave. Our critical task, therefore, involves disenchanting the dominant codes, grappling with how they attempt to control how we "see and act upon reality."[37] According to Wynter, the others' differences are the resources for that rebellion. It is our "very liminality"—she writes—that gives us the edge we need to change social systems.[38]

Another one of Afro-pessimism's inspirations—the Black feminist theorist Hortense Spillers—cautions us against what she calls the "conservative" elements in that formation. In a 2018 discussion at the Institute of Contemporary Arts in London, she remarked:

> I think the afro-pessimistic position really lands in reactionism. It really lands in a deadly, conservative closure. That we stop right here. And that's not what you want to do. I mean you have to get beyond the stop signs, right? You come to a stop. Boom. Hit the brakes and then ok. Then you take off again. I think that's what we have to do with our theorizing.[39]

Here, Spillers imagines a dominant discourse as a stop in the road. The rules of critical engagement mean that we—as thinkers and social actors—must drive past that stop rather than imagine it as a dead end. As she puts it, the dominant code "certainly defines how I am situated in the world that calls me by my name or by whatever other names it's calling me. . . . But I'm not exhausted by that. *I'm that plus!*"[40] For Afro-pessimism to reckon with its conservativism, it would have to identify and create additional equations beyond the one that pairs Blackness with bondage.

To be fair though, a lot of sweat, muscle, hardware, and money have gone into racial domination. Because of this, we shouldn't fault people too much for believing its calculations. Vincent Harding recalled the day when he woke from the lie and began his own process of disenchantment. He was teaching a course at the historically Black Spelman College, arguing that "slavery had dehumanized our people."[41] And then he said,

> That day something moved me to ask myself: who are these young people before me? These are the great-great-grandchildren of those folks I'm saying were dehumanized. If those folks had truly been dehumanized, then these students wouldn't be here. There wouldn't be anybody out there struggling, washing, scrubbing, stealing, hustling to make sure they were here. There would have been no tradition in the family that said, "You've got to be there." There would have been no encouragement that said, "Get out of bed in the morning; you've got to go to school."[42]

"Struggling, washing, scrubbing, stealing, hustling"—we might say that these are the traces of àshe in everyday people. They represent the capacity of neighbors and kin to shape things for *our* better. Such are the powers of the ordinary, the ones unafraid to claim the "enabling light."[43]

The tradition that Harding invokes belongs resolutely to the trickster. As the scholar Trudier Harris notes, "By definition, tricksters are animals or characters who, while ostensibly disadvantaged and weak in a contest of wills, power, and/or resources, succeed in getting the best of their larger, more powerful adversaries."[44] More than the presumed capabilities of might or riches, tricksters believe in their capacity for cunning. In the history of Black peoples, this capacity is both a matter of experience and an article of faith.

Like Harding's story, Smith's drawings are reminders that it is possible to rebound from dehumanization and that social transformation depends on our experiments with recovery. The beauty of Smith's installation and manifesto lies in the fact that the reading list presumes that putting Frantz Fanon with Cherrie Moraga and Fredric Jameson does not corrupt Blackness but potentially refreshes our understanding of it. New juxtapositions like the ones dramatized by the installation create opportunities to experiment with and expand the rescues of Black radical traditions.

Nodding to the need for other codes, equations, and discourses, Smith advocates for a reading list that is ever-changing. She says, "Sincere apologies for obvious omissions—I can't draw or read fast enough. It's gonna have to be a team effort."[45] Since the installation's debut, other catastrophes have bloodied our horizon—the Israeli genocide, the war in Sudan, the US invasion of Venezuela, Israel's bombing of Lebanon, and the Israel-U.S. war against Iran, chief among them. About the genocide of Palestinians, one United Nations report states, "Amid mass killings, eradication of family lines, large-scale targeting of children and torture, the occupied Palestinian territory is being intentionally rendered unliveable—one home, school, church, mosque, hospital, neighbourhood, community, at a time."[46] The war in Sudan has displaced tens of millions of people and established acute food insecurity as the norm for millions more. Mass executions and sexual violence have become routine there. According to one report, the accumulated violence of this war has "provoked one of the world's biggest humanitarian catastrophes."[47] The arrest of President Nicholas Maduro of Venezuela and the wars in Lebanon and Iran represent naked attempts to undermine the sovereignty of other countries and to expand US and Israeli dominance. A reading list that contends with these urgencies might advance an equation like "Blackness = the critique of genocide and empire."

Human__3.0 contains a drawing of Angela Davis's 1981 book *Women, Race, and Class*. The drawing is taken from the edition with the brown cover that has Davis's name and the title in black and bold font (see figure 30). There is a glow that surrounds the name and title, a glow that Smith has colored light yellow. The glow gives the impression of a luminous outline, as if the ensemble "women," "race," and "class" promise the chance for new illuminations. Furthermore, Smith draws a Black or Brown person's thumb touching the bottom left corner of the book. With this, the book becomes an extension of the holder while the reader becomes a segment of the text and the discoveries that it promises. Reader and book, Smith suggests, have the power to re-create one another.

The drawing of Davis's book is made of watercolors and graphite and is drawn on graph paper with traces of glitter glue. If we look closely enough, we can see that the materials reinforce *Human__3.0*'s emphasis on social transformation and indeed imply basic political principles. To begin with, watercolor has been a way for artists to deploy a vast range of colors and hues. Painters have combined its wet and dry paint to produce countless effects—soft edges, hard edges, smooth surfaces, rough surfaces, and so on.[48] With *Human__3.0*, we might think of watercolor as a metaphor for the diverse strategies, tactics, and models that are at our disposal even when the options for social change seem limited.

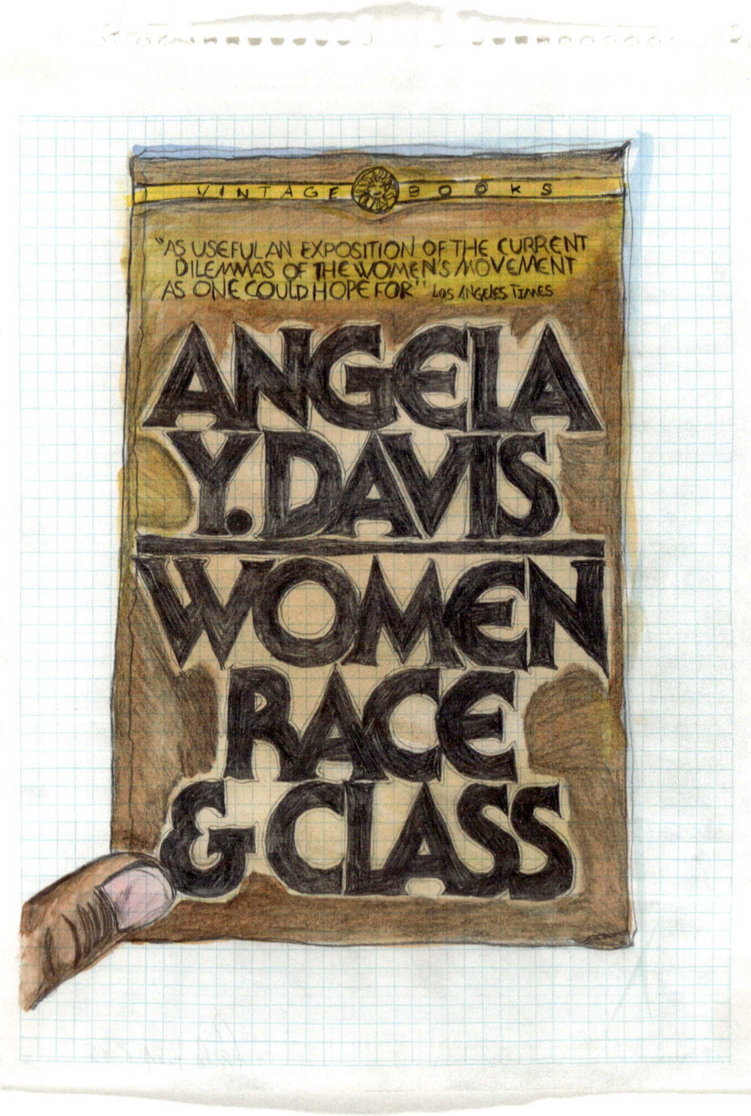

Figure 30. Cauleen Smith. *Angela Y. Davis, Women, Race & Class*. From *Human_3.0 Reading List*. 2015. Graphite and watercolor with traces of glitter glue on wove graph paper. 30 x 21.5 cm (11 13/16 x 8 ½ in.). Art Institute of Chicago, Chicago. Reprinted with permission.

Soft and obliging, graphite is ideal for the message that *Human__3.0* wishes to send as well. Unlike ink and oil, it can be easily removed. As a result, artists, engineers, and mathematicians have used it to make sketches, proposals, and designs that can be revised in the moment.[49] Through *Human__3.0*, it reminds us that novel images, worlds, and structures can take flight from simple markings but should always be open to redrafting.

For decades, engineers have used graph paper to draw and measure spaces—to sketch the mechanical, plumbing, and electrical systems that will go into a building; to document the conditions for various sites; and to brainstorm with architects and other engineers.[50] With this in mind, we might read Smith's use of graph paper as an invitation to assess the conditions for embarking on new and progressive forms of community. Just as engineers use graph paper to provide rigor and structure to their imaginative designs, we too should consider what tools are needed for our own rigorous alternatives.

For her part, Davis gestured toward the co-creative potential of and the disciplined conversations between Black radical traditions and their inheritors. Invoking the enslaved women who endured the terrors of slavery, she wrote, "It was those women who passed on to their nominally free female descendants a legacy of hard work, perseverance and self-reliance, a legacy of tenacity, resistance and insistence on sexual equality—in short, a legacy spelling out standards for a new womanhood."[51] In this legacy, we have the ancestral authorization we need to rewrite the dominant codes and to render images that can open the way.

Acknowledgments

I am fortunate to be the beneficiary of numerous kindnesses. Indeed, many people have escorted me to this book's completion. Jane Blocker, Daisy Bousquet-Desrosiers, Jonathan Flatley, Grace Hong, Katie Lofton, Jason Stanley, Stan Thangaraj, Laura Wexler, and the manuscript's anonymous readers provided invaluable feedback on chapters and lectures. The K-12 teachers who took my seminars on Black art and social struggle with the Yale New Haven Teachers institute and the National Teachers Institute helped me find a language that lay people might hear. Tamar Szabó Gendler introduced me to Sarah Elizabeth Lewis's work on Carrie Mae Weems. The chapter on Weems is all the better because of that phone conversation. I owe a huge debt to Avery Gordon for reading practically every word. Her comments sharpened tremendously the book's analytical and political horizons. Tacey Hutten has proven to be one of the best research assistants I've ever had. It's been a great privilege to work with her. Sincere thanks for excellent copyediting go to Teresa Jesionowski. Richard Morrison has been a source of consistent friendship and visionary editorship. Over half the books that I've written at this point have been tended by his hand.

My writing retreats with Colette Gaiter and then with Gayatri Gopinath, Chandan Reddy, and Stephanie Smallwood have been special times to work out ideas over food and laughter. Several loved ones gave me rooms in their warm homes so that I could steal away and write. For providing beds, desks, and loads of love, my thanks to Jodi Melamed and Tony Peressini, Avery Gordon and Chris Newfield, as well as Lisa Cacho and David Cayoca.

John Lucas and Claudia Rankine as well as Matt Jacobson and Daphne Brooks took me by the arm and helped me settle into a new life. Cajetan Iheka's work on the environment and African cultural production has been a necessary reeducation for me. Alex Halkias's advice from over thirty years ago in graduate school—"Rod, just assume you don't belong"—still guides. My conversations with Katie Lofton are meals in and of themselves—filled with surprises, nourishment, and always, always inspiration. It would be a strange life for me at Yale and on the East Coast if Lisa Lowe weren't here. The Fates were unusually sweet and charitable when they decided to bring us together. Becky Connekin's friendship has been precious and proof that good fortune can come from even a pandemic. Kandice Chuh's early encouragement to keep pursuing other narrative techniques in my scholarship was a true blessing. My walks with Joanne Meyerowitz have been grounding and fortifying, partly derived from the clarity with which she approaches life. I'm also grateful for Grace Hong's comments on the Mutu chapter, especially, and for years of friendship.

For others across the pond, deep gratitude goes to Diana Cain, especially for our conversations about the mysteries and magic of writing. Adrian Rifkin and Denis Echard are dear to me. Whether zoom meetings, teas, walks, or lunches in their garden, I always look forward to our time together with a kid's excitement. Sarah Beddington is someone for whom art, politics, and ethics come together beautifully not only in her work but also in her being.

Gloria Wekker and I were reunited in the summer of 2017. She gave me a copy of her book *White Innocence: Paradoxes of Colonialism and Race* and signed it "in sisterhood," and we've been sisters ever since. M. Jacqui Alexander was perhaps the inspiration for trying to wed the critical and spiritual. I hope she sees the DNA of our friendship in these pages. I am fortunate in that two members of my community in London are also enthusiastic members of my community in New Haven. They are Gail Lewis and Liliane Landor. People who can enrich life in two countries are rare indeed, which has no doubt to do with their uncanny ability to be rooted and mobile at the same time. There are many people in this book, and it is a witness to the divine joys of fellowship.

Notes

Preface

1. Walter Benjamin, *Illuminations: Essays and Reflections* (Boston: Houghton Mifflin Harcourt, 2019).

2. Benjamin, *Illuminations.*

3. Benjamin, *Illuminations.*

4. Benjamin, *Illuminations.*

5. A video interview and profile of artist Stephen Hayes and his work *Cash Crop*, https://www.youtube.com/watch?v=EtpBWiw91ZE&ab_channel=TheGuilfordian.

6. Cheryl Finley, *Committed to Memory: The Art of the Slave Ship Icon (Princeton, NJ: Princeton University Press, 2022)*, 186.

7. Finley, *Committed to Memory*, 184.

8. Maya Deren, *Divine Horsemen: The Living Gods of Haiti* (Kingston, NY: McPherson, 1983).

9. Deren, *Divine Horsemen* .

Introduction: The Fool, the Trickster, and the Power of Áshe

1. Guy Debord, *The Society of the Spectacle* (Glasgow: Good Press, 2021), 14.

2. Karl Marx, *Capital, vol. 1*, trans. Benjamin Fowkes (London: Penguin Books, 1990), 163–77.

3. Marx, *Capital, vol.* 1, 163.

4. Marx, *Capital, vol.* 1, 165.

5. "Modern Culture and Our Destiny," *Présence Africaine*, nos. 8, 9, 10 (June–November 1956): 5.

6. "Modern Culture and Our Destiny," 5.

7. "Modern Culture and Our Destiny," 6.

8. "Modern Culture and Our Destiny," 6.

9. "Modern Culture and Our Destiny," 5.

10. Cedric J. Robinson, *Black Marxism: The Making of the Black Radical Tradition* (Chapel Hill: University of North Carolina Press, 2000).

11. Samella Lewis, *African American Art and Artists* (Los Angeles: University of California Press, 1984), 135.

12. Elizabeth Catlett, "The Negro People and American Art at Mid-Century," in *The Art of Elizabeth Catlett*, ed. Samella Lewis (Sussex, DE: Snowfire Publishing, 2000), 99.

13. Lewis Hyde, *The Gift: Creativity and the Artist in the Modern World* (New York: Vintage, 2007), xvi.

14. Hyde, *The Gift*, xvi.

15. Aimé Césaire, "A Salute to the Third World/ for Leopold Sedar Senghor," in *Aimé Césaire: The Collected Poetry (Berkeley: University of California Press, 1983)*, 351.

16. Okwui Enwezor and Chika Okeke-Agulu, *Contemporary African Art since 1980* (Bologna: Damiani, 2009), 30.

17. Alain Locke, "The New Negro," in *Within the Circle: An Anthology of African American Criticism from the Harlem Renaissance to the Present*, ed. Angelyn Mitchell (Durham, NC: Duke University Press, 1994).

18. Ariana Curtis, "Afro-Latinidad in the Smithsonian's African American Museum Spaces," *Public Historian* 40, no. 3 (August 2018): 287–88.

19. Kobena Mercer, *Travel and See: Black Diaspora Art Practices since the 1980s* (Durham, NC: Duke University Press, 2016), 1.

20. Rotimi Fani-Kayode, "Traces of Ecstasy," in *Rotimi Fani-Kayode and Alex Hirst: Photographs*, ed. Mark Sealy (London: Autograph, 1996), 6.

21. Zanele Muholi, "Faces and Phases," *Transition*, no. 107 (2012): 113.

22. Hyde, *The Gift*, xx.

23. Robert Farris Thompson, *Flash of the Spirit: African and Afro-American Art and Philosophy* (New York: Vintage, 1984), xv.

24. Thompson, *Flash of the Spirit*, 7.

25. Hyde, *The Gift*, xvii.

26. Aristotle, *Nicomachean Ethics* (London: Penguin Books, 2004), 149.

27. As philosopher Stephen Everson argues, "For Aristotle . . . political science is not just a 'science' (an *episteme*) but an 'art' (a *techne*). According to [*Nicomachean Ethics* VI.4,] a *techne* is 'a productive disposition involving a true

account.' . . . To acquire the political art, then, is to acquire a productive disposition—that is, a disposition to produce something." See Stephen Everson, Introduction to *Aristotle: The Politics and the Constitution of Athens*, ed. Stephen Everson (Cambridge: Cambridge University Press, 1996), xxxii.

28. Maya Deren, *Divine Horsemen: The Living Gods of Haiti* (Kingston, NY: Documentext, 2004), 96.

29. Thompson, *Flash of the Spirit*, 19.

1. The Shit, the World, and Their Remaking: Noah Purifoy

1. "Interview of Noah Purifoy," 1990, "UCLA Library | Center for Oral History Research," accessed July 14, 2025, https://oralhistory.library.ucla.edu/catalog/21198-zz0008zm4z?counter=1&q=noah+purifoy.

2. Richard Cándida Smith, "Learning from Watts Towers: Assemblage and Community-Based Art In California," *Oral History (Colchester)* 37, no. 2 (2009): 53–54.

3. "The First International Conference of Negro Writers and Artists, Paris, Sorbonne, 19th–22nd September 1956: Full Account," *Présence Africaine*, no. 24/25 (February–May 1959): 127, https://unesdoc.unesco.org/ark:/48223/pf0000163372, accessed July 14, 2025.

4. California Governor's Commission on the Los Angeles Riots, *Violence in the City—An End or a Beginning? A Report (The McCone Report)* (Los Angeles: The Commission, 1965), 1.

5. California Governor's Commission, *Violence in the City*, 1.

6. California Governor's Commission, *Violence in the City*, 1.

7. Donna Murch, "The Many Meanings of Watts: Black Power, *Wattstax*, and the Carceral State," *OAH Magazine of History* 26, no. 1 (January 1, 2012): 38, https://doi.org/10.1093/oahmag/oar062.

8. Sarah Schrank, *Art and the City: Civic Imagination and Cultural Authority in Los Angeles* (Philadelphia: University of Pennsylvania Press, 2009), 138.

9. Murch, "The Many Meanings of Watts," 38.

10. California Governor's Commission, *Violence in the City*, i.

11. California Governor's Commission, *Violence in the City*, 2.

12. California Governor's Commission, *Violence in the City*, 3.

13. California Governor's Commission, *Violence in the City*, 3.

14. "Guest Editor's Introduction: Visual Culture and Race," *Visual Culture and Race* 39, no. 2 (Summer 2014), https://www-jstor-org.yale.idm.oclc.org/stable/44392734?seq=1, accessed July 13, 2025.

15. "Guest Editor's Introduction: Visual Culture and Race," 2.

16. "Guest Editor's Introduction: Visual Culture and Race," 6.

17. "Interview of Noah Purifoy," UCLA Library | Center for Oral History Research.

18. *66 Signs of Neon* (Los Angeles: 66 Signs of Neon, 1966).

19. Daniel Widener, *Black Arts West: Culture and Struggle in Postwar Los Angeles* (Durham, NC: Duke University Press, 2010), 181–86.

20. "Interview of Noah Purifoy," UCLA Library | Center for Oral History Research.

21. "Interview of Noah Purifoy," UCLA Library | Center for Oral History Research.

22. Lorraine Hansberry, "The Negro Writer and His Roots: Toward a New Romanticism," *Black Scholar* 12, no. 2 (1981): 2–12.

23. Hansberry, "The Negro Writer and His Roots," 7.

24. "The First International Conference of Negro Writers and Artists, Paris, Sorbonne, 19th–22nd September 1956," 4.

25. "The First International Conference of Negro Writers and Artists, Paris, Sorbonne, 19th–22nd September 1956," 4.

26. "The First International Conference of Negro Writers and Artists, Paris, Sorbonne, 19th–22nd September 1956," 4.

27. "Interview of Noah Purifoy," UCLA Library | Center for Oral History Research.

28. Hansberry, "The Negro Writer and His Roots."

29. Karl Marx, *Marx and Engels: Collected Works, vol. 3, Marx and Engels: 1843–44* (Baltimore: Lawrence & Wishart, Project MUSE, 1975), 272.

30. Aimé Césaire, *Discourse on Colonialism* (New York: Monthly Review Press, 2000), 42.

31. Césaire, *Discourse on Colonialism*, 42.

32. Paul Von Blum, "Recovering the Rubble: African American Assemblage Art in Los Angeles," *Journal of Pan African Studies* 4, no. 5 (2011): 249.

33. Carolina A. Miranda, "Noah Purifoy, an Artist Forged by Fire," *Los Angeles Times*, August 13, 2015, https://www.latimes.com/entertainment/arts/la-ca-cm-noah-purifoy-20150816-story.html.

34. "Interview of Noah Purifoy," UCLA Library | Center for Oral History Research.

35. Carol Vogel, "Pedestals Standing on Their Own," *New York Times*, July 15, 1982, sec. Home & Garden, https://www.nytimes.com/1982/07/15/garden/pedestals-standing-on-their-own.html.

36. William Chapin Seitz, *Art of Assemblage* (New York: Museum of Modern Art, 1961), 83.

37. Seitz, *Art of Assemblage*, 83.

38. Seitz, *Art of Assemblage*, 83.

39. Widener, *Black Arts West*, 164.
40. "Interview of Noah Purifoy," UCLA Library | Center for Oral History Research.
41. *66 Signs of Neon* (Los Angeles: 66 Signs of Neon, 1966).
42. California Governor's Commission, *Violence in the City*, 3.
43. Karl Marx, *Capital: A Critique of Political Economy*, volume 1 (London: Penguin Books, 1990), 748.
44. James Baldwin, *The Price of the Ticket: Collected Nonfiction, 1948–1985* (New York: St. Martin's/Marek, 1985), 349.
45. "The First International Conference of Negro Writers and Artists, Paris, Sorbonne, 19th–22nd September 1956," 5.
46. Noah Purifoy, *Noah Purifoy: High Desert* (Göttingen, Germany: Steidl, 1997), 7).
47. Smith, "Learning from Watts Towers," 54.
48. John Dewey, *Art as Experience* (Penguin Random House, 2005), 45.
49. Aristotle, *The Nicomachean Ethics*, trans. J. A. K. Thomson, rev. Hugh Tredennick, introduction by Jonathan Barnes (New York: Penguin Random House, 2004), 149.
50. Franklin Sirmans and Yael Lipschutz, eds., *Noah Purifoy: Junk Dada* (Los Angeles, CA: Los Angeles County Museum of Art, 2015), 48.
51. Sirmans and Lipschutz, *Noah Purifoy*.

2. Civilizing Missions and *The Hampton Project*: Carrie Mae Weems

1. Sarah Elizabeth Lewis and Christine Garnier, *Carrie Mae Weems* (Cambridge, MA: MIT Press, 2021).
2. Denise Ramzy and Katherine Fogg, "Interview with Carrie Mae Weems," in *Carrie Mae Weems: The Hampton Project*, by Vivian Patterson (New York: Aperture; Williamstown, MA: Williams College Museum of Art, 2000), 78.
3. Lewis and Garnier, *Carrie Mae Weems*.
4. Vivan Patterson, *Carrie Mae Weems: The Hampton Project* (New York: Aperture; Williamstown, MA: Williams College Museum of Art, 2000), 77.
5. Lewis and Garnier, *Carrie Mae Weems*, 145.
6. Gary Y. Okihiro, *Island World: A History of Hawai'i and the United States* (Berkeley: University of California Press, 2008), 99.
7. Donal F. Lindsey, *Indians at Hampton Institute, 1877–1923* (Urbana: University of Illinois Press, 1995), 3.
8. Lindsey, *Indians at Hampton Institute*, 1.
9. Lindsey, *Indians at Hampton Institute*, 7–9.
10. Lindsey, *Indians at Hampton Institute*, 9.

11. James D. Anderson, *The Education of Blacks in the South, 1860–1935* (Chapel Hill: University of North Carolina Press, 1988), 37.

12. Anderson, *The Education of Blacks in the South*, 42.

13. Anderson, *The Education of Blacks in the South*, 37.

14. Anderson, *The Education of Blacks in the South*, 37.

15. W. E. B. Du Bois, *Black Reconstruction in America, 1860–1880* (New York: Free Press, 1998), 76.

16. Du Bois, *Black Reconstruction in America*, 77.

17. Du Bois, *Black Reconstruction in America*, 664.

18. Colonel Richard P. Hallowell, as quoted in Du Bois, *Black Reconstruction in America*, 664.

19. Lewis and Garnier, *Carrie Mae Weems*, 46.

20. Frances Benjamin Johnston, *The Hampton Album: 44 Photographs from an Album of Hampton Institute* (New York: Museum of Modern Art; distributed by Doubleday, 1966), 22.

21. Johnston, *The Hampton Album*, 22.

22. Ramzy and Fogg, "Interview with Carrie Mae Weems," 78.

23. Ramzy and Fogg, "Interview with Carrie Mae Weems," 78.

24. Michael Robert Patterson, "Richard Henry Pratt—Brigadier General, United States Army," *Arlington National Cemetery* (blog), August 15, 2023, https://www.arlingtoncemetery.net/rhpratt.htm.

25. Paulette Fairbanks Molin, "'Training the Hand, the Head, and the Heart': Indian Education at Hampton Institute," *Minnesota History* 51, no. 3 (1988): 85.

26. Lindsey, *Indians at Hampton Institute*.

27. Lindsey, *Indians at Hampton Institute*.

28. Molin, "Training the Hand, the Head, and the Heart," 84.

29. Molin, "Training the Hand, the Head, and the Heart," 91.

30. Molin, "Training the Hand, the Head, and the Heart," 91.

31. Daniel J. Sharfstein, "'We Only Ask an Even Chance to Live as Other Men Live,'" *Slate*, May 24, 2017, https://slate.com/news-and-politics/2017/05/how-chief-joseph-of-the-nez-perce-became-a-hero-of-civil-rights-advocates.html.

32. Sharfstein, "'We Only Ask an Even Chance to Live as Other Men Live.'"

33. "*Baptism of Indians by Mormons*—St. George, Utah.—Photographs—Huntington Digital Library," https://hdl.huntington.org/digital/collection/p15150coll2/id/10719, accessed August 12, 2023.

34. Sarah Barringer Gordon and Jan Shipps, "Fatal Convergence in the Kingdom of God: The Mountain Meadows Massacre in American History," *Journal of the Early Republic* 37, no. 2 (2017): 335.

35. See Martin A. Berger, *Sight Unseen: Whiteness and American Visual Culture* (Berkeley: University of California Press, 2005).

36. Lewis and Garnier, *Carrie Mae Weems*, 19–20.

37. Lewis and Garnier, *Carrie Mae Weems*, 16.

38. Laura Wexler, *Tender Violence: Domestic Visions in an Age of US Imperialism*. Chapel Hill: University of North Carolina Press, 2000.

39. Suzan Sherman, "Carrie Mae Weems's *The Hampton Project*," *Bomb Magazine*, https://bombmagazine.org/articles/carrie-mae-weemss-the-hampton-project/, accessed March 13, 2024.

40. Lindsey, *Indians at Hampton Institute*, 35.

41. Lindsey, *Indians at Hampton Institute*, 35.

42. Lindsey, *Indians at Hampton Institute*, 19.

43. Lindsey, *Indians at Hampton Institute*, 23.

44. Lindsey, *Indians at Hampton Institute*, 23–24.

45. Chloé Wolifson, "The Textile Turn in Contemporary Art," *Art Monthly Australasia*, no. 339 (June 2024): 32–39.

46. Molin, "Training the Hand, the Head, and the Heart," 95.

47. Molin, "Training the Hand, the Head, and the Heart," 95.

48. Molin, "Training the Hand, the Head, and the Heart," 86.

49. Immanuel Kant, *The Conflict of the Faculties*, trans. Mary J. Gregor (Lincoln: University of Nebraska Press, 1992), 23.

50. H. B. Frissell, *The Hampton Normal and Agricultural Institute and Its Work for Negro and Indian Youth* (Hampton: Hampton Institute, 1898), 10.

51. Captain R. H. Pratt, "The Advantages of Mingling Indians with Whites," in *Proceedings of the National Conference of Charities and Correction at the Ninth Annual Session Held in Denver, Colorado, June 23–29, 1892*, ed. Isabel C. Barrows, https://carlisleindian.dickinson.edu/teach/kill-indian-him-and-save-man-r-h-pratt-education-native-americans. Accessed 11//5/21.

52. Patterson, *Carrie Mae Weems*, 78.

53. "Indian Labor," *Virginia Star*, November 11, 1882. Author unknown.

54. "Indian Labor," *Virginia Star*, November 11, 1882.

55. "Indian Labor," *Virginia Star*, November 11, 1882.

56. "Indian Labor," *Virginia Star*, November 11, 1882.

57. Frissell, *The Hampton Normal and Agricultural Institute*, 10.

58. Frissell, *The Hampton Normal and Agricultural Institute*, 10.

59. Kyle T. Mays, *An Afro-Indigenous History of the United States* (Boston: Beacon Press, 2021), xvii.

60. Mays, *An Afro-Indigenous History*, xvii.

61. Sonia Ashmore, *Muslin* (New York: Harry N. Abrams, 2012), 24.

62. Dawoud Bey, "Carrie Mae Weems," in *Carrie Mae Weems*, ed. Sarah Elizabeth Lewis with Christine Garnier (Cambridge, MA: MIT Press, 2021), 150.

63. Patterson, *Carrie Mae Weems*, 78.

64. Vincent Harding, "Responsibilities of the Black Scholar to the Community," *The State of Afro-American History: Past, Present, and Future*, ed. Darlene Clark Hine (Baton Rouge: Louisiana State University Press, 1986), 278.

65. Harding, "Responsibilities of the Black Scholar to the Community," 278.

66. Anna Bender, "Quital's First Hunt," in *Recovering Native American Writings in the Boarding School Press* (Lincoln: University of Nebraska Press, 2017), 134.

67. Bender, "Quital's First Hunt," 134.

68. Nick Estes, *Our History Is the Future: Standing Rock versus the Dakota Access Pipeline, and the Long Tradition of Indigenous Resistance* (New York: Verso, 2019), 15.

69. Estes, *Our History Is the Future*, 254.

70. Patterson, *Carrie Mae Weems*, 80.

71. Estes, *Our History Is the Future*, 14.

3. The Sea as History and Prophecy: Hew Locke, John Akomfrah, Fabrice Monteiro

1. *For Those in Peril on the Sea*, Pérez Art Museum, https://www.sothebys.com/en/museums/perez-art-museum-miami/exhibitions/for-those-in-peril-on-the-sea, accessed June 17, 2025.

2. Pérez Art Museum Miami: Project Gallery: Hew Locke, https://www.youtube.com/watch?v=QcKgNmUngnc&ab_channel=P%C3%A9rezArtMuseumMiami, accessed November 4, 2021.

3. Hymnary.org, "Eternal Father, Strong to Save," https://hymnary.org/text/eternal_father_strong_to_save_whose_arm. Accessed November 4, 2021.

4. Hymnary.org, "Eternal Father, Strong to Save."

5. Pérez Art Museum.

6. Louisa Buck, "Hew Locke Discusses Monarchy and Model Boats in New Survey Show at Ikon Gallery," March 11, 2019, https://www.theartnewspaper.com/2019/03/11/hew-locke-discusses-monarchy-and-model-boats-in-new-survey-show-at-ikon-gallery.

7. Charles Henry Rowell and Hew Locke, "An Interview with Hew Locke," *Callaloo* 37, no. 3 (Summer 2014): 529.

8. Stuart Hall and David Morley, *Essential Essays, vol. 2, Stuart Hall* (Durham, NC: Duke University Press, 2018), 319.

9. Hall and Morley, *Essential Essays*, vol. 2, *Stuart Hall*, 320.

10. Hall and Morley, *Essential Essays*, vol. 2, *Stuart Hall*, 101.

11. Hall and Morley, *Essential Essays*, vol. 2, *Stuart Hall*, 101.

12. Iain Chambers, "War on the Water," in the catalog for *Sink without a Trace: Exhibition on Migrant Deaths at Sea* (London: P21 Gallery, 2019), 40.

13. Pérez Art Museum.

14. Laleh Khalili, *Sinews of War and Trade: Shipping and Capitalism in the Arabian Peninsula* (London: Verso, 2021), 236.

15. Khalili, *Sinews of War and Trade*, 237.

16. Khalili, *Sinews of War and Trade*, 238.

17. Sharon Ottoman and Mark McDonald, "Highjacked Supertanker Anchors Off Somalia," *New York Times*, November 18, 2008. https://www.nytimes.com/2008/11/19/world/africa/19pirate.html. Accessed May 8, 2020.

18. For a history of how pirates have been criminalized, see Peter Linebaugh and Marcus Rediker, *The Many-Headed Hydra: Sailors, Slaves, Commoners, and the Hidden History of the Revolutionary Atlantic* (Boston: Beacon Press, 2013).

19. Khadija Sharife, "Flying a Questionable Flag: Liberia's Lucrative Shipping Industry," *Reportage* (Winter 2010/2011): 118.

20. Nicholas de Genova, "The 'Migrant Crisis' as Racial Crisis: Do *Black Lives Matter* in Europe?" *Ethnic and Racial Studies* 41, no.10 (2018): 1766–67.

21. Claire Bishop, *Installation Art: A Critical History* (New York: Routledge, 2005), 13.

22. Buck,"Hew Locke Discusses Monarchy and Model Boats."

23. Clara Sankey and Lindsey Westbrook, "An Interview with John Akomfrah," SFMOMA, July 2018, https://www.sfmoma.org/read/interview-john-akomfrah/. Accessed 3/18/20.

24. Allan Sekula, *Fish Story* (Düsseldorf: Richter Verlag, 1995), 43.

25. For a discussion of how Grotius constructed the Portuguese as pirates, see Michael Kempe, "Beyond the Law: The Image of Piracy in the Legal Writings of Hugo Grotius," *Gratiana* 26–28 (2005–2007): 379–95.

26. Hugo Grotius, *The Freedom of the Seas or the Right Which Belongs to the Dutch to Take Part in the East Indian Trade*, trans. Ralph van Deman Magoffin (New York: Oxford University Press, 1918), 4.

27. Grotius, *The Freedom of the Seas*, 7.

28. Grotius, *The Freedom of the Seas*, 8.

29. Markus Vink, "'The World's Oldest Trade': Dutch Slavery and Slave Trade in the Indian Ocean in the Seventeenth Century," *Journal of World History* 14, no. 2 (June 2003):, 132.

30. Stephanie E. Smallwood, *Saltwater Slavery: A Middle Passage from Africa to American Diaspora* (Cambridge, MA: Harvard University Press, 2008), 17–18.

31. Christina Sharpe, *In the Wake: On Blackness and Being* (Durham, NC: Duke University Press, 2018), 21.

32. Molly Rogers, *Delia's Tears: Race, Science, and Photography in Nineteenth-Century America* (New Haven, CT: Yale University Press, 2010), 17–21.

33. Derek Walcott, *The Poetry of Derek Walcott, 1948–2013* (New York: Macmillan, 2014), 253.

34. Walcott, *The Poetry of Derek Walcott*, 253.

35. Sekula, *Fish Story*, 12.

36. Walcott, *The Poetry of Derek Walcott*, 253.

37. Sekula, *Fish Story*, 12.

38. Smallwood, *Saltwater Slavery*, 68. Also for a similar argument see Marcus Rediker, *The Slave Ship: A Human History* (New York: Viking, 2007).

39. Sankey and Westbrook, "An Interview with John Akomfrah."

40. Sankey and Westbrook, "An Interview with John Akomfrah."

41. Walcott, *The Poetry of Derek Walcott*, 253.

42. Sankey and Westbrook, "An Interview with John Akomfrah."

43. Cedric J. Robinson, *Black Marxism: The Making of the Black Radical Tradition* (Chapel Hill: University of North Carolina Press, 1983), 171.

44. For a similar argument in experimental form, see Alexis Pauline Gumbs, *M Archive: After the End of the World* (Durham, NC: Duke University Press, 2018).

45. Cajetan Iheka, *Naturalizing Africa: Ecological Violence, Agency, and Postcolonial Resistance in African Literature* (Cambridge: Cambridge University, 2018), 9.

46. Iheka, *Naturalizing Africa*, 5.

47. David Naguib Pellow, *Resisting Global Toxics: Transnational Movements for Environmental Justice* (Cambridge, MA: MIT Press, 2007), 38.

48. Christian Neidan, "The Photographic Confrontations of Fabrice Monteiro: An Interview," https://www.themantle.com/arts-and-culture/photographic-confrontations-fabrice-monteiro-interview. Accessed July 7, 2020.

49. Neidan, "The Photographic Confrontations of Fabrice Monteiro."

50. Neidan, "The Photographic Confrontations of Fabrice Monteiro."

51. John S. Mbiti, *Introduction to African Religion*, 2nd ed. (Long Grove, IL: Waveland Press, 2015), 70.

52. Mbiti, *Introduction to African Religion*, 72.

53. Iheka, *Naturalizing Africa*, 12.

54. Michael Watts, "Oil City: Petro-Landscapes and Sustainable Futures," in *African Cities Reader II: Mobilities and Fixtures*, ed. Ntone Edjabe and Edgar Pieterse (Chimurenga: African Centre for Cities, 2011), 93.

55. Watts, "Oil City," 95.

56. Watts, "Oil City," 95.

57. André Bazin, "The Ontology of the Photographic Image," in *Classic Essays on Photography*, ed. Alan Trachtenberg (New Haven, CT: Leete's Island Books, 1980), 241.

58. Susan Sontag, *On Photography* (New York: Picador, 1977), 15.

59. Sandra Laville, "Dumped Fishing Gear Is Biggest Plastic Polluter in Ocean, Finds Report," *The Guardian*, November 5, 2019, https://www.theguardian.com/environment/2019/nov/06/dumped-fishing-gear-is-biggest-plastic-polluter-in-ocean-finds-report. Accessed September 6, 2020.

60. Emma Bryce, "'An Invisible Killer': How Fishing Gear became the Deadliest Marine Plastic," *The Guardian*, November 7, 2022, https://www.theguardian.com/environment/2022/nov/07/invisible-killer-ghost-fishing-gear-deadliest-marine-plastic.

61. Greenpeace, "Ghost Gear: The Abandoned Fishing Nets Haunting Our Oceans," 5, https://www.greenpeace.org/aotearoa/publication/ghost-gear-the-abandoned-fishing-nets-haunting-our-oceans/.

62. Greenpeace, "Ghost Gear."

63. Nancy Hall-Duncan, *The History of Fashion Photography* (New York: Alpine, 1979), 99.

64. Robin D. G. Kelley, *Freedom Dreams: The Black Radical Imagination* (New York: Random House, 2000), 158.

65. Suzanne Césaire, *The Great Camouflage: Writings of Dissent (1941–1945)* (Middletown, CT: Wesleyan University, 2012), 35.

66. Kelley, *Freedom Dreams*, 159.

67. Cheikh Tidiane Sylla, "Surrealism and Black African Art," in *Black, Brown, and Beige: Surrealist Writings from Africa and the Diaspora*, ed. Franklin Rosemont and Robin D. G. Kelley (Austin: University of Texas Press, 2009), 181.

68. Paul Griffin, "Carbon Majors Database: CDP Carbon Majors Report 2017," 8, https://www.cdp.net/en/articles/media/new-report-shows-just-100-companies-are-source-of-over-70-of-emissions.

69. Griffin, "Carbon Majors Database," 7.

70. Françoise Vergès, "Racial Capitalocene," in *Futures of Black Radicalism*, ed. Gaye Theresa Johnson and Alex Lubin (London: Verso, 2017), 77. See also Mike Davis, *Late Victorian Holocausts: El Niño Families and the Making of the Third World* (London: Verso, 2001).

71. Walter Rodney, *How Europe Underdeveloped Africa* (Brooklyn, NY: Verso, 2018), 212.

72. Vergès, "Racial Capitalocene."

4. Mutations of Militarism and War: Wangechi Mutu

1. Wangechi Mutu, "The Power of Earth in My Work: Essay for the Smithsonian National Museum of African Art," https://africa.si.edu/exhibits/earthmatters/quotes/mutu.html, accessed June 18, 2025.

2. Wangechi Mutu, "The Power of Earth in My Work."

3. Wangechi Mutu, "The Power of Earth in My Work."

4. Wangechi Mutu, "The Power of Earth in My Work."

5. Wangechi Mutu, "The Power of Earth in My Work."

6. Wangechi Mutu, "The Power of Earth in My Work."

7. "East African Commission (Report)—Hansard—UK Parliament," 6–7, https://hansard.parliament.uk/Commons/1925-04-29/debates/b367016f-87c8-4f59-aa31-0201151e6753/EastAfricanCommission(Report), accessed June 18, 2025.

8. "East African Commission(Report)—Hansard—UK Parliament," 7.

9. "East African Commission (Report)—Hansard—UK Parliament," 22.

10. "East African Commission (Report)—Hansard—UK Parliament," 23.

11. "East African Commission (Report)—Hansard—UK Parliament," 22.

12. See Caroline Elkins, *Imperial Reckoning: The Untold Story of Britain's Gulag in Kenya* (New York: Henry Holt, 2005).

13. For a history of these organizations, see Anthony Howarth and David R. Koff's documentary *The Black Man's Land Trilogy* (1973), particularly episode 2, "Mau Mau."

14. Caroline Elkins, *Imperial Reckoning: The Untold Story of Britain's Gulag in Kenya* (New York: Henry Holt, 2005), xi.

15. Elkins, *Imperial Reckoning.*

16. Elkins, *Imperial Reckoning*, xiii.

17. Elkins, *Imperial Reckoning.*

18. Elkins, *Imperial Reckoning*, xvi.

19. Elkins, *Imperial Reckoning*, xvi.

20. Amina Mama and Margo Okazawa-Rey, "Militarism, Conflict and Women's Activism in the Global Era: Challenges and Prospects for Women in Three West African Contexts," *Feminist Review*, no. 101 (2012): 9.

21. Mama and Okazawa-Rey, "Militarism, Conflict and Women's Activism in the Global Era."

22. Kristine Stiles, "Wangechi Mutu's Family Tree," in *Wangechi Mutu: A Fantastic Journey*, ed. Trevor Schoonmaker (Durham, NC: Nasher Museum of Art, Duke University, 2013), 64.

23. Mama and Okazawa-Rey, "Militarism, Conflict and Women's Activism in the Global Era," 98.

24. Trevor Schoonmaker, "Wangechi Mutu: A Fantastic Journey," *Nka: Journal of Contemporary African Art*, no. 35 (Fall 2014): 48.
25. Harry G. West and Stacy Sharpes, "Dealing with the Devil: Meaning and the Marketplace in Makonde Sculpture," *African Arts* 35, no. 3 (2002): 36.
26. Julius K. Nyerere, *Ujamaa—Essays on Socialism* (London: Oxford University Press, 1977), 12.
27. Mama and Okazawa-Rey, "Militarism, Conflict and Women's Activism in the Global Era," 99.
28. Mama and Okazawa-Rey, "Militarism, Conflict and Women's Activism in the Global Era," 99.
29. Schoonmaker, "Wangechi Mutu: A Fantastic Journey," 48.
30. Mama and Okazawa-Rey, "Militarism, Conflict and Women's Activism in the Global Era," 101.
31. Schoonmaker, "Wangechi Mutu: A Fantastic Journey," 48.
32. For a discussion of how Mutu's work manipulates beauty, see Zakiyyah Iman Jackson, *Becoming Human: Matter and Meaning in an Antiblack World* (New York: NYU Press, 2020).
33. Daniel Burland, "War and Militarism," in *The Cambridge Handbook of Social Problems*, ed. A. Javier Treviño (Cambridge: Cambridge University Press, 2018), 2:147, https://doi.org/10.1017/9781108550710.010.
34. Frantz Fanon, *The Wretched of the Earth* (New York: Grove Press, 1968), 147.
35. Fanon, *The Wretched of the Earth*, 147.
36. Fanon, *The Wretched of the Earth*, 35.
37. Fanon, *The Wretched of the Earth*, 36.
38. Mama and Okazawa-Rey, "Militarism, Conflict and Women's Activism in the Global Era," 99.
39. Aaronette M. White, "All the Men Are Fighting for Freedom, All the Women Are Mourning Their Men, but Some of Us Carried Guns: A Raced-Gendered Analysis of Fanon's Psychological Perspectives on War," *Signs* 32, no. 4 (2007): 874, https://doi.org/10.1086/513021.
40. Mama and Okazawa-Rey, "Militarism, Conflict and Women's Activism in the Global Era," 101.
41. Mama and Okazawa-Rey, "Militarism, Conflict and Women's Activism in the Global Era," 3.
42. Priya Lal, *African Socialism in Postcolonial Tanzania between the Village and the World* (Cambridge: Cambridge University Press, 2015), 83.
43. Lal, *African Socialism in Postcolonial Tanzania*, 82.
44. Lal, *African Socialism in Postcolonial Tanzania*, 81.

45. Lal, *African Socialism in Postcolonial Tanzania*, 84.
46. White, "All the Men Are Fighting for Freedom," 879.
47. White, "All the Men Are Fighting for Freedom," 865.
48. White, "All the Men Are Fighting for Freedom," 875.
49. Jillian Hernandez, "The Ambivalent Grotesque: Reading Black Women's Erotic Corporeality in Wangechi Mutu's Work," *Signs* 42, no. 2 (2017): 446.
50. Michel Foucault, *Discipline and Punish: The Birth of the Prison* (New York: Vintage Books, 1977), 136.
51. Foucault, *Discipline and Punish*, 135.
52. Jennifer James, "War," in *Keywords for African American Studies*, ed. Erica R. Edwards, Roderick A. Ferguson, and Jeffrey O. G. Ogbar (New York: NYU Press, 2018), 217.
53. Quoted in White, "All the Men Are Fighting for Freedom," in Consortium on *Gender, Security, and Human Rights*, https://genderandsecurity.org/projects-resources/working-papers/all-men-are-fighting-freedom-all-women-are-mourning-their-men-some. Working Paper No. 302/2006, 22. PDF download.
54. White, Working Paper No. 302/2006, 17.
55. White, Working Paper No. 302/2006, 17.
56. White, Working Paper No. 302/2006, 18.
57. Grigory Yevseyevich Zinovyev, *Socialism and War* (New York: International, 1933), 9.
58. White, Working Paper No. 302/2006, 20.
59. White, Working Paper No. 302/2006, 20.
60. White, Working Paper No. 302/2006, 20.
61. White, Working Paper No. 302/2006, 19.
62. Stiles, "Wangechi Mutu's Family Tree," 51.
63. Holland Cotter, "A Window, Not a Mirror," Arts, *New York Times*, October 10, 2013, https://www.nytimes.com/2013/10/11/arts/design/a-survey-of-wangechi-mutu-at-brooklyn-museum.html.
64. Conflict and Environment Observatory, "How Does War Damage the Environment?" June 4, 2020. https://ceobs.org/how-does-war-damage-the-environment/. Accessed 1/21/22.
65. Conflict and Environment Observatory, "How Does War Damage the Environment?"
66. Conflict and Environment Observatory, "How Does War Damage the Environment?"
67. Conflict and Environment Observatory, "How Does War Damage the Environment?"
68. Conflict and Environment Observatory, "How Does War Damage the Environment?"

69. James, "War," 217.

70. James, "War," 217.

71. Carl von Clausewitz, *On War*, ed. and trans. Michael Howard and Peter Paret (New York: Knopf, 1993), 83.

72. James, "War," 216.

73. Roderick A. Ferguson, "Untitled," unpublished poem, 2024.

Conclusion: To Make Things Happen

1. Cauleen Smith, *Human 3.0 Reading List 2015–2016* (Chicago: Corbette vs. Dempsey, 2016); Kimberlé Crenshaw, *#SayHerName: Black Women's Stories of Police Violence and Public Silence (Chicago: Haymarket Press, 2023)*; and Donald Cohen and Mikaelian Allen, *The Privatization of Everything: How the Plunder of Public Goods Changed America and How We Can Fight Back (New York:New Press, 2021)*.

2. Cohen and Allen, *The Privatization of Everything*.

3. Smith, *Human 3.0 Reading List 2015–2016*, 67.

4. Smith, manifesto.

5. Susan Owens, *The Story of Drawing: An Alternative History of Art* (New Haven, CT: Yale University Press, 2024), 7.

6. Owens, *The Story of Drawing*, 6.

7. György Lukács, *History and Class Consciousness (Cambridge, MA: MIT Press, 1971)*, 39.

8. Lukács, *History and Class Consciousness*, 39.

9. Michael Hardt and Antonio Negri, *The Labour of Dionysus: A Critique of the State-Form (Minneapolis: University of Minnesota Press*, 1994), 6.

10. Smith, *Human 3.0 Reading List 2015–2016*, 65.

11. Owens, *The Story of Drawing*, 6.

12. Frederick Douglass, *The Life and Times of Frederick Douglass* (New York: Collier Books, 1962), 84.

13. Douglass, *Life and Times of Frederick Douglass*, 85.

14. Douglass, *Life and Times of Frederick Douglass*, 85. Douglass attributes the speech about the lust for power as the origin of oppression to Richard Brinsley Sheridan, but it's more likely that he meant the Irish revolutionary Arthur O'Connor. See Patrice J. Ferreira, "Frederick Douglass in Ireland: The Dublin Edition of His *Narrative*," *New Hibernia Review* 5, no. 1 (Spring 2001): 53–67.

15. Malcolm X, *The Autobiography of Malcolm X (New York: Grove Press, 1965)*.

16. Joseph Beam, "Introduction: Leaving the Shadows Behind," in *In the Life: A Black Gay Anthology*, ed. Joseph Beam (Boston: Alyson Publications, 1986), 13.

17. Beam, "Introduction: Leaving the Shadows Behind," 13.

18. Mary Helen Washington, Foreword to *Their Eyes Were Watching God: A Novel*, by Zora Neale Hurston (New York: Perennial Library, 1990), 9.

19. Washington, Foreword to *Their Eyes Were Watching God*, xiv.

20. Jeff R. Donaldson, "AfriCOBRA Manifesto? Ten in Search of a Nation," *Nka: Journal of Contemporary African Art* 30 (Spring 2012): 81.

21. See Wadsworth A. Jarrell, *AfriCobra: Experimental Art Toward a School of Thought* (Durham, NC: Duke University Press, 2020).

22. BLK Art Group, "Radical Black Art: A Working Convention Programme," chrome-extension://efaidnbmnnnibpcajpcglclefindmkaj/https://cms.nottinghamcontemporary.org/site/assets/files/4448/radicalblackartsworkingconvention1984.pdf#:~:text=This%20convention%20was%20organised%20by,common%20commitment%20to%20the%20development. Accessed April 5, 2026.

23. Samella Lewis, *African American Art and Artists*. Los Angeles: University of California Press, 1984.

24. Elizabeth Catlett, "The Role of the Black Artist," *Black Scholar* 42, no. 2 (June 1, 2012): 45, https://doi.org/10.5816/blackscholar.42.2.0041.

25. Catlett, "The Role of the Black Artist," 45.

26. Catlett, "The Role of the Black Artist," 45.

27. Smith, *Human 3.0 Reading List 2015–2016*, 67.

28. Smith, *Human 3.0 Reading List 2015–2016*, 67.

29. Frank B. Wilderson III, "Afro-Pessimism and the End of Redemption," Humanities Futures, Franklin Humanities Institute, Duke University. October 20, 2015. https://humanitiesfutures.org/papers/afro-pessimism-end-redemption/index.html.

30. Wilderson, "Afro-Pessimism and the End of Redemption."

31. Sylvia Wynter, "On Disenchanting Discourse: 'Minority' Literary Criticism and Beyond," *Cultural Critique*, no. 7 (1987): 221.

32. Wynter, "On Disenchanting Discourse," 222.

33. Wynter, "On Disenchanting Discourse," 216.

34. Wynter, "On Disenchanting Discourse," 216.

35. Wynter, "On Disenchanting Discourse," 228.

36. Wynter, "On Disenchanting Discourse," 235.

37. Wynter, "On Disenchanting Discourse," 220.

38. Wynter, "On Disenchanting Discourse," 235,

39. Institute of Contemporary Arts, "Hortense Spillers and Gail Lewis at the Institute of Contemporary Arts," June 25, 2018, https://www.youtube.com/watch?v=tQoORQqSaWU&t=4346s.

40. Institute of Contemporary Arts, "Hortense Spillers and Gail Lewis at the Institute of Contemporary Arts."

41. MARHO: The Radical Historians Organization, ed., "Vincent Harding," in *Visions of History* (New York: Pantheon, 1984), 235.

42. MARHO: The Radical Historians Organization, ed., "Vincent Harding," 235.

43. Robert Farris Thompson, *Flash of the Spirit: African and Afro-American Art and Philosophy* (New York: Vintage Books, 1984), 5. Thompson argued that the Yoruba supreme god Olurun made àshe available to human beings and described it as "God's enabling light."

44. Trudier Harris, "The Trickster in African American Literature, Freedom's Story," TeacherServe®, National Humanities Center, https://nationalhumanities center.org/tserve/freedom/1865-1917/essays/trickster.htm. Accessed June 25, 2025.

45. Smith, *Human 3.0 Reading List 2015–2016*, 68.

46. United Nations, General Assembly, Report of the Special Rapporteur on the Situation of Human Rights in the Palestinian Territories, "Genocide as Colonial Erasure" (New York: UN Headquarters, 2024), 22.

47. Human Rights Watch, "Sudan: Events of 2024." https://www.hrw.org /world-report/2025/country-chapters/sudan. Accessed April 8, 2026.

48. Metropolitan Museum of Art, "Materials and Techniques: Watercolors," https://www.metmuseum.org/perspectives/materials-and-techniques-drawing -watercolor.Accessed April 8, 2026.

49. Metropolitan Museum of Art, "Materials and Techniques: Graphite," https://www.metmuseum.org/perspectives/materials-and-techniques-drawing -graphite. Accessed April 8, 2026.

50. Pat's Blog, "Notes on the History of Graph Paper," October 30, 2023, https://pballew.blogspot.com/2023/10/notes-on-history-of-graph-paper.html. Accessed April 8, 2026.

51. Angela Y. Davis, *Women, Race, and Class (New York: Vintage, 1983)*, 29.

Bibliography

Anderson, James D. *The Education of Blacks in the South, 1860–1935*. Chapel Hill: University of North Carolina Press, 1988.

Aristotle. *The Nicomachean Ethics*. Translated by J. A. Thomson; revised by Hugh Tredennick; with an introduction by Jonathan Barnes. New York: Penguin Random House, 2004.

Ashmore, Sonia. *Muslin*. New York: Harry N. Abrams, 2012.

Baldwin, James. *The Price of the Ticket: Collected Nonfiction, 1948–1985*. New York: St. Martin's/Marek, 1985.

Baptism of Indians by Mormons. St. George, Utah. Photographs. Huntington Digital Library. https://hdl.huntington.org/digital/collection/p15150coll2/id/10719. Accessed August 12, 2023,

Bazin, André. "The Ontology of the Photographic Image." In *Classic Essays on Photography*, edited by Alan Trachtenberg. New Haven, CT: Leete's Island Books, 1980.

Beam, Joseph. "Introduction: Leaving the Shadows Behind." In *In the Life: A Black Gay Anthology*, edited by Joseph Beam. Boston: Alyson Publications, 1986.

Bender, Anna. "Quital's First Hunt." In *Recovering Native American Writings in the Boarding School Press. Lincoln*: University of Nebraska Press, 2017.

Benjamin, Walter. *Illuminations: Essays and Reflections*. Boston: Houghton Mifflin Harcourt, 2019.

Berger, Martin A. *Sight Unseen: Whiteness and American Visual Culture*. Berkeley: University of California Press, 2005.

Bishop, Claire. *Installation Art: A Critical History*. New York: Routledge, 2005.
BLK Art Group, "Radical Black Art: A Working Convention Programme." chrome-extension://efaidnbmnnnibpcajpcglclefindmkaj/https://cms.nottinghamcontemporary.org/site/assets/files/4448/radicalblackartsworkingconvention1984.pdf#:~:text=This%20convention%20was%20organised%20by,common%20commitment%20to%20the%20development. Accessed April 5, 2026.
Buck, Louisa. "Hew Locke Discusses Monarchy and Model Boats in New Survey Show at Ikon Gallery." *The Art Newspaper*, March 11, 2019. https://www.theartnewspaper.com/2019/03/11/hew-locke-discusses-monarchy-and-model-boats-in-new-survey-show-at-ikon-gallery.
Burland, Daniel. "War and Militarism." In *The Cambridge Handbook of Social Problems*. Vol. 2. Edited by A. Javier Treviño. Cambridge: Cambridge University Press, 2018. https://doi.org/10.1017/9781108550710.010.
California Governor's Commission on the Los Angeles Riots. *Violence in the City—An End or a Beginning? A Report*. The McCone Report. Los Angeles: The Commission, 1965.
Cándida Smith, Richard. "Learning from Watts Towers: Assemblage and Community-Based Art in California." *Oral History (Colchester)* 37, no. 2 (2009): 53–54.
Captain R. H. Pratt. "The Advantages of Mingling Indians with Whites." In *Proceedings of the National Conference of Charities and Correction at the Ninth Annual Session Held in Denver, Colorado, June 23–29, 1892*, edited by Isabel C. Barrows. https://carlisleindian.dickinson.edu/teach/kill-indian-him-and-save-man-r-h-pratt-education-native-americans. Accessed 11//5/21.
Catlett, Elizabeth, "The Negro People and American Art at Mid-Century." In *The Art of Elizabeth Catlett, edited by Samella Lewis*. Sussex, DE: Snowfire Publishing, 2000.
Catlett, Elizabeth. "The Role of the Black Artist." *Black Scholar* 42, no. 2 (June 1, 2012): 45. https://doi.org/10.5816/blackscholar.42.2.0041.
Césaire, Aimé. *Discourse on Colonialism*. New York: Monthly Review Press, 2000.
Césaire, Aimé. "A Salute to the Third World/ for Leopold Sedar Senghor." In *Aimé Césaire: The Collected Poetry, translated by Clay Eshleman and Annette Smith. Berkeley: University of California Press, 1983.*
Césaire, Suzanne. *The Great Camouflage: Writings of Dissent (1941–1945)*. Middletown, CT: Wesleyan University, 2012.
Chambers, Iain "War on the Water." In the catalog for *Sink without a Trace: Exhibition on Migrant Deaths at Sea*. London: P21 Gallery, 2019.
Clausewitz, Carl von. *On War. Edited and translated by* Michael Howard and Peter Paret. New York: Knopf, 1993.

Cohen, Donald, and Mikaelian Allen, *The Privatization of Everything: How the Plunder of Public Goods Changed America and How We Can Fight Back. New York: New Press, 2021.*

Conflict and Environment Observatory. "How Does War Damage the Environment?" June 4, 2020. https://ceobs.org/how-does-war-damage-the-environment/. Accessed 1/21/22.

Cotter, Holland. "A Window, Not a Mirror." *New York Times*, October 10, 2013, sec. Arts. https://www.nytimes.com/2013/10/11/arts/design/a-survey-of-wangechi-mutu-at-brooklyn-museum.html.

Crenshaw, Kimberlé. *#SayHerName: Black Women's Stories of Police Violence and Public Silence. Chicago: Haymarket Press, 2023.*

Curtis, Ariana. "Afro-Latinidad in the Smithsonian's African American Museum Spaces." *Public Historian* 40, no. 3 (August 2018).

Davis, Angela Y. *Women, Race, and Class*. New York: Vintage, 1983,

Davis, Mike. *Late Victorian Holocausts: El Niño Families and the Making of the Third World*. London: Verso, 2001.

Debord, Guy. *The Society of the Spectacle*. Glasgow: Good Press, 2021.

De Genova, Nicholas. "The 'Migrant Crisis' as Racial Crisis: Do *Black Lives Matter* in Europe?" *Ethnic and Racial Studies* 41, no. 10 (2018): 1765–82.

Deren, Maya. *Divine Horsemen: The Living Gods of Haiti*. Kingston, NY: McPherson, 1983.

Dewey, John. *Art as Experience*. New York: Penguin, 2005.

Donaldson, Jeff R. "AfriCOBRA Manifesto? Ten in Search of a Nation." *Nka: Journal of Contemporary African Art* 30 (Spring 2012).

Douglass, Frederick. *The Life and Times of Frederick Douglass*. New York: Collier Books, 1962.

Du Bois, W. E. B., and David Levering Lewis. *Black Reconstruction in America, 1860–1880*. New York: Free Press, 1998.

"East African Commission(Report)—Hansard—UK Parliament," 6–7, https://hansard.parliament.uk/Commons/1925-04-29/debates/b367016f-87c8-4f59-aa31-0201151e6753/EastAfricanCommission(Report). Accessed June 18, 2025.

Elkins, Caroline. *Imperial Reckoning: The Untold Story of Britain's Gulag in Kenya*. New York: Henry Holt, 2005.

Enwezor, Okwui, and Chika Okeke-Agulu. *Contemporary African Art since 1980*. Bologna: Damiani, 2009.

Estes, Nick. *Our History Is the Future: Standing Rock versus the Dakota Access Pipeline, and the Long Tradition of Indigenous Resistance*. New York: Verso, 2019.

Everson, Stephen. Introduction to *Aristotle: The Politics and the Constitution of Athens*, ed. Stephen Everson. Cambridge: Cambridge University Press, 1996.

Fani-Kayode, Rotimi. "Traces of Ecstasy." In *Rotimi Fani-Kayode and Alex Hirst: Photographs*, edited by Mark Sealy. London: Autograph, 1996.
Fanon, Frantz. *The Wretched of the Earth*. New York: Grove Press, 1968.
Ferguson, Roderick A. "Untitled." Unpublished poem, 2024.
Ferreira, Patrice J. "Frederick Douglass in Ireland: the Dublin Edition of His *Narrative*." *New Hibernia Review* 5, no. 1 (Spring 2001): 53–67.
Finley, Cheryl. *Committed to Memory: The Art of the Slave Ship Icon*. Princeton, NJ: Princeton University Press, 2022.
"The First International Conference of Negro Writers and Artists, Paris, Sorbonne, 19th–22nd September 1956: Full Account." *Présence Africaine*, no. 24/25 (February–May 1959): 127. https://unesdoc.unesco.org/ark:/48223/pf0000163372. Accessed July 14, 2025.
Foucault, Michel. *Discipline and Punish: The Birth of the Prison*. New York: Vintage Books, 1977.
Frissell, H. B. *The Hampton Normal and Agricultural Institute and Its Work for Negro and Indian Youth*. India: Pranava Books.
Gordon, Sarah Barringer, and Jan Shipps. "Fatal Convergence in the Kingdom of God: The Mountain Meadows Massacre in American History." *Journal of the Early Republic* 37, no. 2 (2017).
Greenpeace. "Ghost Gear: The Abandoned Fishing Nets Haunting Our Oceans." https://www.greenpeace.org/aotearoa/publication/ghost-gear-the-abandoned-fishing-nets-haunting-our-oceans/.
Griffin, Paul. "Carbon Majors Database: CDP Carbon Majors Report 2017." https://www.cdp.net/en/articles/media/new-report-shows-just-100-companies-are-source-of-over-70-of-emissions.
Grotius, Hugo. *The Freedom of the Seas or the Right Which Belongs to the Dutch to Take Part in the East Indian Trade*. Translated by Ralph van Deman Magoffin. New York: Oxford University Press, 1918.
"Guest Editor's Introduction: Visual Culture and Race on JSTOR." https://www.jstor-org.yale.idm.oclc.org/stable/44392734?seq=1. Accessed July 13, 2025.
Gumbs, Alexis Pauline. *M Archive: After the End of the World*. Durham, NC: Duke University Press, 2018.
Hall, Stuart, and David Morley. *Essential Essays. Vol. 2: Stuart Hall*. Durham, NC: Duke University Press, 2018.
Hall-Duncan, Nancy. *The History of Fashion Photography*. New York: Alpine, 1979.
Hansberry, Lorraine. "The Negro Writer and His Roots: Toward a New Romanticism." *Black Scholar* 12, no. 2 (1981).
Harding, Vincent. In *The State of Afro-American History?: Past, Present, and Future*, edited by Darlene Clark Hine. Baton Rouge: Louisiana State University Press, 1986.

Hardt, Michael, and Antonio Negri. *The Labour of Dionysus: A Critique of the State-Form. Minneapolis: University of Minnesota Press, 1994.*

Harris, Trudier. "The Trickster in African American Literature, Freedom's Story." TeacherServe®, National Humanities Center. https://nationalhumanitiescenter.org/tserve/freedom/1865-1917/essays/trickster.htm. Accessed June 25, 2025.

Hernandez, Jillian. "The Ambivalent Grotesque: Reading Black Women's Erotic Corporeality in Wangechi Mutu's Work." *Signs* 42, no. 2 (2017).

Howarth, Anthony, and David Koff. *The Black Man's Land Trilogy.* Anthony David Productions, Inc., 1973.

Human Rights Watch, "Sudan: Events of 2024." https://www.hrw.org/world-report/2025/country-chapters/sudan. Accessed April 8, 2026.

Hyde, Lewis. *The Gift: Creativity and the Artist in the Modern World.* New York: Vintage, 2007.

Hymnary.org, "Eternal Father, Strong to Save." https://hymnary.org/text/eternal_father_strong_to_save_whose_arm. Accessed November 4, 2021.

Iheka, Cajetan. *Naturalizing Africa: Ecological Violence, Agency, and Postcolonial Resistance in African Literature.* Cambridge: Cambridge University Press, 2018,

"Indian Labor." *Virginia Star,* November 11, 1882. Author unknown.

Institute of Contemporary Arts. "Hortense Spillers and Gail Lewis at the Institute of Contemporary Arts." June 25, 2018. https://www.youtube.com/watch?v=tQoORQqSaWU&t=4346s.

"Interview of Noah Purifoy." 1990. UCLA Library, Center for Oral History Research. https://oralhistory.library.ucla.edu/catalog/21198-zz0008zm4z?counter=1&q=noah+purifoy. Accessed July 14, 2025.

Jackson, Zakiyyah Iman. *Becoming Human: Matter and Meaning in an Antiblack World.* New York: NYU Press, 2020.

James, Jennifer. "War." In *Keywords for African American Studies,* edited by Erica R. Edwards, Roderick A. Ferguson, and Jeffrey O. G. Ogbar. New York: NYU Press, 2018.

Jarrell, Wadsworth A. *AfriCobra: Experimental Art Toward a School of Thought.* Durham, NC: Duke University Press, 2020.

Johnston, Frances Benjamin. *The Hampton Album: 44 Photographs from an Album of Hampton Institute.* New York: Museum of Modern Art; distributed by Doubleday, 1966.

66 Signs of Neon. Los Angeles: 66 Signs of Neon, 1966.

Kant, Immanuel. *The Conflict of the Faculties.* Translated with an introduction by Mary J. Gregor. Lincoln: University of Nebraska Press, 1992.

Kelley, Robin D. G. *Freedom Dreams: The Black Radical Imagination.* New York: Random House, 2000.

Kempe, Michael. "Beyond the Law: The Image of Piracy in the Legal Writings of Hugo Grotius." *Gratiana* 26–28 (2005–2007): 379–95.

Laleh. *Sinews of War and Trade: Shipping and Capitalism in the Arabian Peninsula*. London: Verso, 2021.

Lal, Priya. *African Socialism in Postcolonial Tanzania between the Village and the World*. New York: Cambridge University Press, 2015.

Laville, Sandra, "Dumped Fishing Gear Is Biggest Plastic Polluter in Ocean, Finds Report." *The Guardian*, November 5, 2019. https://www.theguardian.com/environment/2019/nov/06/dumped-fishing-gear-is-biggest-plastic-polluter-in-ocean-finds-report. Accessed September 6, 2020.

Lewis, Samella. *African American Art and Artists*. Los Angeles: University of California Press, 1984.

Lewis, Sarah Elizabeth, and Christine Garnier. *Carrie Mae Weems*. Cambridge, MA: MIT Press, 2021.

Lindsey, Donal F. *Indians at Hampton Institute, 1877–1923*. Urbana: University of Illinois Press, 1995.

Linebaugh, Peter, and Marcus Rediker. *The Many-Headed Hydra: Sailors, Slaves, Commoners, and the Hidden History of the Revolutionary Atlantic*. Boston: Beacon Press, 2013.

Locke, Alain. "The New Negro." In *Within the Circle: An Anthology of African American Criticism from the Harlem Renaissance to the Present*, edited by Angelyn Mitchell. Durham, NC: Duke University Press, 1994.

Lukács, György. *History and Class Consciousness*. Cambridge, MA: MIT Press, 1971.

Malcolm X, *The Autobiography of Malcolm X. New York: Grove Press, 1965.*

Mama, Amina, and Margo Okazawa-Rey. "Militarism, Conflict and Women's Activism in the Global Era: Challenges and Prospects for Women in Three West African Contexts." *Feminist Review*, no. 101 (2012).

MARHO: The Radical Historians Organization, ed. "Vincent Harding." In *Visions of History*. New York: Pantheon, 1984.

Marx, Karl. *Capital, vol. 1*. Translated by Benjamin Fowkes. London: Penguin Books, 1990.

Marx, Karl. *Marx & Engels Collected Works. Vol. 3: Marx and Engels: 1843–44*. London: Lawrence & Wishart; Baltimore: Project MUSE, 1975.

Mays, Kyle T. *An Afro-Indigenous History of the United States*. Boston: Beacon Press, 2021.

Mbiti, John S. *Introduction to African Religion*. 2nd ed. Long Grove, IL: Waveland Press, 2015.

Mercer, Kobena. *Travel and See: Black Diaspora Art Practices since the 1980s*. Durham, NC: Duke University Press, 2016.

Metropolitan Museum of Art. "Materials and Techniques: Graphite." https://www.metmuseum.org/perspectives/materials-and-techniques-drawing-graphite. Accessed April 8, 2026.

Metropolitan Museum of Art. "Materials and Techniques: Watercolors." https://www.metmuseum.org/perspectives/materials-and-techniques-drawing-watercolor. Accessed April 8, 2026.

Miranda, Carolina A. "Noah Purifoy, an Artist Forged by Fire." *Los Angeles Times*, August 13, 2015. https://www.latimes.com/entertainment/arts/la-ca-cm-noah-purifoy-20150816-story.html.

"Modern Culture and Our Destiny." *Présence Africaine*, nos. 8, 9, 10 (June–November 1956).

Molin, Paulette Fairbanks. "'Training the Hand, the Head, and the Heart': Indian Education at Hampton Institute." *Minnesota History* 51, no. 3 (1988).

Muholi, Zanele. "Faces and Phases." *Transition, no.* 107 (2012): 112–24. https://muse.jhu.edu/article/465737.

Murch, Donna. "The Many Meanings of Watts: Black Power, *Wattstax*, and the Carceral State." *OAH Magazine of History 26, no. 1* (January 1, 2012): 37–40. https://doi.org/10.1093/oahmag/oar062.

Mutu, Wangechi. "The Power of Earth in My Work: Essay for the Smithsonian National Museum of African Art." https://africa.si.edu/exhibits/earthmatters/quotes/mutu.html. Accessed June 18, 2025.

Neidan, Christian. "The Photographic Confrontations of Fabrice Monteiro: An Interview."

Nyerere, Julius K. *Ujamaa—Essays on Socialism*. London: Oxford University Press, 1977.

Okihiro, Gary Y. *Island World: A History of Hawai'i and the United States*. Berkeley: University of California Press, 2008.

Ottoman, Sharon, and Mark McDonald. "Highjacked Supertanker Anchors Off Somalia." *New York Times*, November 18, 2008. https://www.nytimes.com/2008/11/19/world/africa/19pirate.html. Accessed May 8, 2020.

Owens, Susan. *The Story of Drawing: An Alternative History of Art*. New Haven, CT: Yale University Press, 2024.

Pat's Blog. "Notes on the History of Graph Paper." October 30, 2023. https://pballew.blogspot.com/2023/10/notes-on-history-of-graph-paper.html. Accessed April 8, 2026.

Patterson, Michael Robert. "Richard Henry Pratt—Brigadier General, United States Army." *Arlington National Cemetery* (blog), August 15, 2023. https://www.arlingtoncemetery.net/rhpratt.htm.

Patterson, Vivian. *Carrie Mae Weems: The Hampton Project*. New York: Aperture; Williamstown, MA: Williams College Museum of Art, 2000.

Pellow, David Naguib. *Resisting Global Toxics: Transnational Movements for Environmental Justice*. Cambridge, MA: MIT Press, 2007.

Pérez Art Museum. *For Those in Peril on the Sea*. https://www.sothebys.com/en/museums/perez-art-museum-miami/exhibitions/for-those-in-peril-on-the-sea. Accessed June 17, 2025.

Pérez Art Museum Miami: Project Gallery: Hew Locke. https://www.youtube.com/watch?v=QcKgNmUngnc&ab_channel=P%C3%A9rezArtMuseumMiami. Accessed November 4, 2021.

Pratt, Captain R. H. "The Advantages of Mingling Indians with Whites." In *Proceedings of the National Conference of Charities and Correction at the Ninth Annual Session Held in Denver, Colorado, June 23–29, 1892*, edited by Isabel C. Barrows. https://carlisleindian.dickinson.edu/teach/kill-indian-him-and-save-man-r-h-pratt-education-native-americans. Accessed November 5, 2021.

Noah Purifoy, Noah. *Noah Purifoy: High Desert*. Göttingen, Germany: Steidl, 1997.

Ramzy, Denise, and Katherine Fogg. "Interview with Carrie Mae Weems." In *Carrie Mae Weems: The Hampton Project*, by Vivian Patterson. New York: Aperture; Williamstown, MA: Williams College Museum of Art, 2000.

Rediker, Marcus. *The Slave Ship: A Human History*. New York: Viking, 2007.

Robinson, Cedric J. *Black Marxism: The Making of the Black Radical Tradition*. Chapel Hill: University of North Carolina Press, 2000.

Rodney, Walter. *How Europe Underdeveloped Africa*. Brooklyn, NY: Verso, 2018.

Rogers, Molly. *Delia's Tears: Race, Science, and Photography in Nineteenth-Century America*. New Haven, CT: Yale University Press, 2010.

Rowell, Charles Henry, and Hew Locke. "An Interview with Hew Locke." *Callaloo* 37, no. 3 (Summer 2014): 524–40.

Sankey, Clara, and Lindsey Westbrook. "An Interview with John Akomfrah." SFMOMA, July 2018. https://www.sfmoma.org/read/interview-john-akomfrah/. Accessed March 18, 2020.

Schoonmaker, Trevor. "Wangechi Mutu: A Fantastic Journey." *Nka: Journal of Contemporary African Art*, no. 35 (Fall 2014): 42–53.

Schrank, Sarah. *Art and the City Civic Imagination and Cultural Authority in Los Angeles*. Philadelphia: University of Pennsylvania Press, 2009.

Seitz, William Chapin. *Art of Assemblage*. New York: Museum of Modern Art, 1961.

Sekula, Allan. *Fish Story*. Düsseldorf: Richter Verlag, 1995.

Sharfstein, Daniel J. "We Only Ask an Even Chance to Live as Other Men Live." *Slate*, May 24, 2017. https://slate.com/news-and-politics/2017/05/how-chief-joseph-of-the-nez-perce-became-a-hero-of-civil-rights-advocates.html.

Sharife, Khadija. "Flying a Questionable Flag: Liberia's Lucrative Shipping Industry." *Reportage* (Winter 2010/2011): 111–18.
Sharpe, Christina. *In the Wake: On Blackness and Being*. Durham, NC: Duke University Press, 2018.
Sherman, Suzan. "Carrie Mae Weems's *The Hampton Project*." *Bomb Magazine*, Spring 2001. https://bombmagazine.org/articles/carrie-mae-weemss-the-hampton-project/. Accessed March 13, 2024.
Sirmans, Franklin, and Yael Lipschutz, eds. *Noah Purifoy: Junk Dada*. Los Angeles, CA: Los Angeles County Museum of Art, 2015.
66 Signs of Neon. Los Angeles: 66 Signs of Neon, 1966.
Smallwood, Stephanie E. *Saltwater Slavery: A Middle Passage from Africa to American Diaspora*. Cambridge, MA: Harvard University Press, 2008.
Smith, Cauleen. *Human 3.0 Reading List 2015–2016*. Chicago: Corbette vs. Dempsey, 2016.
Sontag, Susan. *On Photography*. New York: Picador, 1977.
Stiles, Kristine. "Wangechi Mutu's Family Tree." In *Wangechi Mutu: A Fantastic Journey*, edited by Trevor Schoonmaker. Durham, NC: Nasher Museum of Art, Duke University, 2013.
Sylla, Cheikh Tidiane. "Surrealism and Black African Art." In *Black, Brown, and Beige: Surrealist Writings from Africa and the Diaspora*, edited by Franklin Rosemont and Robin D. G. Kelley. Austin: University of Texas Press, 2009.
Thompson, Robert Farris. *Flash of the Spirit: African and Afro-American Art and Philosophy*. New York: Vintage, 1984.
United Nations, General Assembly. Report of the Special Rapporteur on the Situation of Human Rights in the Palestinian Territories. "Genocide as Colonial Erasure." New York: UN Headquarters, 2024.
Vergès, Françoise. "Racial Capitalocene." In *Futures of Black Radicalism*, edited by Gaye Theresa Johnson and Alex Lubin. London: Verso, 2017.
Vink, Markus. "'The World's Oldest Trade': Dutch Slavery and Slave Trade in the Indian Ocean in the Seventeenth Century." *Journal of World History* 14, no. 2 (June 2003): 131–77.
Vogel, Carol. "Pedestals Standing on Their Own." *New York Times*, July 15, 1982, sec. Home & Garden. https://www.nytimes.com/1982/07/15/garden/pedestals-standing-on-their-own.html.
Von Blum, Paul, "Recovering the Rubble: African American Assemblage Art in Los Angeles." *Journal of Pan African Studies* 4, no. 5 (2011).
Walcott, Derek. *The Poetry of Derek Walcott, 1948–2013*. New York: Macmillan, 2014.
Washington, Mary Helen. Foreword to *Their Eyes Were Watching God: A Novel*, by Zora Neale Hurston. New York: Perennial Library, 1990.

Watts, Michael. "Oil City: Petro-Landscapes and Sustainable Futures." In *African Cities Reader II: Mobilities and Fixtures,* edited by Ntone Edjabe and Edgar Pieterse. Chimurenga: African Centre for Cities, 2011.

West, Harry G., and Stacy Sharpes. "Dealing with the Devil: Meaning and the Marketplace in Makonde Sculpture." *African Arts* 35, no. 3 (2002).

Wexler, Laura. *Tender Violence: Domestic Visions in an Age of US Imperialism.* Chapel Hill: University of North Carolina Press, 2000.

White, Aaronette M. "All the Men Are Fighting for Freedom, All the Women Are Mourning Their Men, but Some of Us Carried Guns: A Raced-Gendered Analysis of Fanon's Psychological Perspectives on War." *Signs* 32, no. 4 (2007): 874. https://doi.org/10.1086/513021.

Widener, Daniel. *Black Arts West? Culture and Struggle in Postwar Los Angeles.* Durham, NC: Duke University Press, 2010.

Wilderson, Frank B, III. "Afro-Pessimism and the End of Redemption." Humanities Futures, Franklin Humanities Institute, Duke University. October 20, 2015. https://humanitiesfutures.org/papers/afro-pessimism-end-redemption/index.html.

Wolifson, Chloé. "The Textile Turn in Contemporary Art." *Art Monthly Australasia*, no. 339 (June 2024): 32–39.

Sylvia Wynter. "On Disenchanting Discourse: 'Minority' Literary Criticism and Beyond." *Cultural Critique*, no. 7 (Autumn 1987): 207–44.

Zinovyev, Grigory Yevseyevich. *Socialism and War.* New York: International, 1933.

Roderick A. Ferguson is the William Robertson Coe Professor of Women's, Gender, and Sexuality Studies and American Studies at Yale University. He is the author of *One-Dimensional Queer, We Demand: The University and Student Protests, The Reorder of Things: The University and Its Pedagogies of Minority Difference,* and *Aberrations in Black: Toward a Queer of Color Critique.*